Fan-Tastic:
The Love Behind The Vent
An Intimate Memoir

Penny Milks
with Lois Gilbert

Fan-Tastic: The Love Behind The Vent
An Intimate Memoir

Copyright © 2010 by (Penny Milks)

Printed in the United States of America

ISBN 9-780984-569908

First Edition: June 2010

To my husband Stephen, who made me laugh
and see the world through his eyes.
You will always be my true love.
Love you forever.

Acknowledgement

So many loved ones have helped Steve and me along the way and I am humbled by your dedication. You know who you are, and the role you played in our lives. Thank you for your affection and support.

Milks Family, you hold a special place in my heart and I'm happy to be part of your family.

Mother and Dad, I love you and thank you for always loving me.

Tammie, you have been the one constant throughout my life. You have always been there and I am glad you are my sister and my friend.

Steph and Stevie, we have been through tremendous changes in our lives over the past four years. I am proud you are my children, my friends and my allies.

To the women in my life, I cherish and love every one of you. Each of you has played an important role in my growth and helped me become the woman I am today.

Perry, you were Steve's best friend and bud and I'm honored to have you as my friend and bud.

Jaybird, as Steve so fondly called you, I treasure our friendship, and I'm grateful for your help and late night rescue missions. Steve loved you like a brother and he would be giving you a big thumbs up.

A special thanks to Dr. Ron. Your kindness, support and love during Steve's illness went beyond the call of duty. I'm privileged to have you as my doctor and my friend.

Tonya, where do I begin? You are my glue. You have been by my side through good and bad times. You cried with me, laughed with me and laughed at me. You listened to me and watched as I went through each stage of the grieving and recovery process. You heard the Steve stories time after time, yet you still managed to smile through them. I love you like a sister, Steve loved you like a daughter and it is no wonder he nicknamed you Mighty Mouse.

Dedication

In the spring of 2009, I searched the internet for an editor who would help me complete my memoir, and found Lois Gilbert's website. Just as Steve and I were destined to cross paths, I believe Lois and I were fated to meet each other. What began as a review of my manuscript became an amazing journey that I never could have anticipated.

Lois lost her brother Steve to cancer in January, 2006, and three months later, cancer claimed my Steve. Although Lois and I live in different states, thousands of miles apart, we both knew the same heartbreak, and we'd both been shattered by loss.

Our journey started simply: write a love story, chronicled by my memories. As our correspondence broadened, we found we had more in common than death and bereavement. We admired the strength, discipline and humor we found in each other, and our daily work on the memoir helped us develop a bond that quickly bloomed into friendship.

Lois has my undying gratitude for turning my labor of love into her labor of love. She questioned me and prodded me with patience, compassion and empathy for what I'd lived through. She jogged my memories to bring my story alive with her gift and flair for words. Because of her talent, I can relive the passion of my history with Steve, simply by picking up our book.

This chapter of my journey with Lois has ended. What remains is our friendship, and a new and deeper chapter in our lives has begun.

Fan-Tastic:
The Love Behind The Vent
An Intimate Memoir

Foreword

This is a love story. Not just any love story; it is my love story. It may seem like an ordinary tale to most people. There is nothing earth-shattering about it, yet it shattered my earth.

Have you ever met someone and known in the deepest part of yourself that you'd met your soul mate? The bond between two people can be so strong that you only have to look at each other to know what the other one is feeling and thinking.

I met that person, my mate, my best friend and the love of my life. Steve is gone now, and I'm left with an ache like no other in the bottom of my heart. Who am I without him? I write this for myself and our children and grandchildren, to remember the years that Steve and I shared, and perhaps to heal the pain in my heart.

❧ Chapter One ❧

Our story begins in September 1974 in a small town outside of Kansas City, Missouri. Just a week after my eighteenth birthday, a sandy-haired stranger swaggered into the RV dealership where I worked, and the manager bustled in behind him. We all sat up a little straighter as we registered the crackle of energy that radiated from the blond man who grinned at all of us like he already owned the place. Dressed in jeans and a periwinkle-blue shirt that echoed the color of his eyes, he was a handsome, arresting figure. My senses went on full alert as I took in the broad shoulders that tapered to a narrow waist, a trim backside and the wiry legs of a cowboy. *Who was he?* Even back then, I had the feeling he was Somebody.

The manager beamed at him. "This is Steve Milks, everybody. He's joining our sales staff, and I hope you all help him learn the ropes around here."

Whoa, I thought, *he sure is good-looking.* The stranger's gaze swept the room until it came to rest on me, and his left eyebrow quirked up—interested or amused by my homemade clothes, I couldn't tell. I blushed, tried to pull the hem of my miniskirt down over my knees and hid behind the curtain of my hair.

The new salesman walked directly over to my chair to stand before me.

"Glad to be here." His gaze lingered on me, and the grin never left his face as his blue eyes twinkled. I could feel the heat rise in my cheeks as he took his time studying me, from the toes of my Mary Janes to the long, straight brown hair that framed my face.

When Steve reached out to shake my hand I gulped and accidentally swallowed my gum, and it formed a knot in my throat that only added to my discomfort as he grasped my sweaty palm. His hands were strong, his nails manicured, and his paw swallowed mine as if he'd like to hold on forever.

An uncomfortable silence ensued as Steve gravely pumped my hand up and down, as if he could pump out a greeting from my stricken throat. I knew my face was blazing red.

"Seems like the stick shift on this baby has a nice smooth action," he said as he pumped my arm. "And so far I'd say she's a real quiet ride." He cut his eyes back to the other men in the room, and they burst out laughing.

I tried to pull my hand away from his grasp, but Steve held on tight. His eyes were merry, bright with mischief, and even though I was miserable at being singled out, those eyes hypnotized me. Looking into them felt like I was staring into the bottomless depths of a sky-blue ocean that might drown me. Pinned to the spot by his gaze, I fought back a wave of vertigo and swallowed hard to get the gum down.

"What's your name, sweet pea?" he asked.

"Penny," I said, barely above a whisper. I yanked my hand out of his and hid both hands behind my back so he wouldn't grab me again. While he stood there grinning at me I wanted to dig a hole, crawl in it and pull the hole in after me.

"Hi, Penny," he whispered in a perfect imitation of me. "I hope your voice comes back real soon."

The roar of laughter from the other men in the room annoyed me, but I was used to being on the receiving end of their good-old-boy humor. As the only girl in the men's club of the dealership, I was often the butt of their jokes. The owner's wife protected me from most of the harassment, but back in those days women in the workplace were expected to put up with a certain amount of unwanted attention from their male co-workers. When I went into the dealership to apply for the position of sales clerk, the manager asked me to stand up and turn around, and that's all it took to get the job.

The noise of the men's laughter brought the owner's wife to the doorway. "Quit teasing that poor girl," she said, but her mouth twitched with the desire to smile. "She looks like she's having a heart attack."

Steve looked deep into my eyes, placed one hand on his chest and shook his head. "She's the one who started it, Mrs. C. She stole my heart, and I'm just trying to get it back."

By now I felt like my face was on fire. "You can have your heart back." I pushed my glasses up on my nose and gave him my haughtiest look. "I've got no use for it."

The room erupted in whistles and shouts, and Steve finally backed away from me, palms up.

Was it love at first sight? Hardly. In fact, it was just the opposite. He picked on me relentlessly. He was sarcastic, poked fun at my accent and mimicked the way I said "I reckon so," "t'weren't" and "y'all." My mother's people were from Arkansas, and I'd spent so many holidays with them that my pronunciation of everyday words had a distinctive southern lilt. Now the accent

I grew up with and thought perfectly normal suddenly made me so self-conscious I could hardly open my mouth around him. *How dare he make fun of my southern drawl and call me a hillbilly!* I left work swearing I hated him.

When my boyfriend Jerome came by the dealership to drive me home he took one look at Steve and his lips tightened in a grim line.

"Who's the new guy?" he asked as soon as I shut the car door.

"His name is Steve. Steve Milks."

Jerome glanced in the rearview mirror at the cluster of salesmen who were grouped around Steve in the lot. Steve was born to be the center of attention, with the quick wit of a class clown coupled with a sharp intelligence no one could miss— and then there were those Steve McQueen eyes, that beautiful body, and the way he made me feel like I was talking to a movie star. Jerome was only sixteen, and Steve had to be at least twice his age.

Jerome gave me a worried glance. "He looks like trouble to me."

Yeah, you're probably right, I thought. "Believe me, you've got nothing to worry about. He's a real smart aleck." I fiddled with the knob of the radio to search for my favorite station. The airwaves were full of news commentators discussing Nixon's resignation a few weeks before, and it made me uneasy to listen to them. The U.S. had finally pulled out of Vietnam the year before, and the country seemed to be waking up from a bad hangover.

Finally I found a station playing "Time in a Bottle," and I

settled back in the seat to sink into Jim Croce's soothing voice and watch the gently rolling farmland outside my open window.

I was born in Wichita, Kansas, but my family moved to Liberty, Missouri—a town just outside of Kansas City—when I was three years old. One of the main employment opportunities in Liberty was the Hallmark greeting card distribution center. My mom worked there, and my sister went to work there after she graduated.

Until I met Steve, I never imagined that I would leave. This was the heartland of America. We felt like we were the real deal, the true citizens of the American Dream. To those of us born here in the middle of the country, it felt like the center of the universe. Kansas City was a top distributor of food and farm machinery to the rest of the world, and churned out automobiles, trucks, electrical equipment, steel and vending machines. The city looked like a starburst on the map, with blue lines of trunk line railways and highways radiating out in all directions, while the Mississippi River ran right through the middle of town. There was a symphony orchestra, an opera company, a Federal Reserve Bank, several colleges and universities, and one of the most elegant residential districts in the country. Why go anywhere else when the world came to our doorstep?

"I have a bad feeling about that new guy." Jerome drummed his fingers against the steering wheel as he darted an anxious look at me. "You stay away from him, you hear? A guy like that wouldn't think twice about taking advantage of you."

I rolled my eyes and turned up the volume on the radio. It was a warm day, more like August than September, and the heat clung to the streets as we drove to Wilshire Estates, the subdivision where I'd grown up. My sister Tammie ran out to greet us as we pulled into the driveway, while our Boston terrier Mitsy careened toward us and jumped, twirled and tried to lick my face as soon as I stepped out of the car.

"Thanks for the ride," I called out as I slammed the car door. "Talk to you later, okay?"

Jerome looked surprised. "You don't want me to come in?"

I shrugged. "I'm pretty tired. It was a rough day." I felt guilty for the indifference I felt, but the truth was that Jerome suddenly looked like a boy to me, compared to the man I'd met that day. Fickle as a weathervane, my hormones seemed to halt in mid-stream and surge toward the memory of how Steve's hand felt when it swallowed mine. What would those hands feel like if he drew me closer?

When Jerome drove away Tammie watched me with big eyes, alert to the change in me even though I hadn't said a word to her. "What's the matter with you? Don't you like him anymore?"

"Sure I like him," I said. "I just want to be alone, that's all."

"Are you sick?"

"No, Toad, I'm not sick. Don't you have homework to do?"

She studied me for a moment, clearly intrigued by the difference she saw in me, and then she shrugged and ran into the house. I stopped to scratch Mitsy behind her ears before I walked slowly up the path to the front door. Tammie was right. I did feel different. It seemed like I'd spent my whole life growing up in the safe harbor of my family, and I'd never had the chance to travel or explore anywhere else. Was that about to change?

A wistful nostalgia for the life I'd led up until now flooded through me, and suddenly I felt homesick for it, as if I were already on the deck of a big ship that was pulling me away from the familiarity of the past and heading out toward uncharted waters. This time next year, where would I be? I could be anywhere, and that thought made me feel anxious.

When I entered the house I could see Mother in the kitchen, looking trim as usual in her tank top and polyester slacks, her hands a blur as she chopped up tomatoes and cucumbers for dinner. My dad usually slept until he had to get up for his midnight shift at TWA, where he worked as a mechanic. Pretty soon Tammie, Mother and I would eat dinner, then we'd sit around in the rec room downstairs to watch *All in the Family*.

I shook off the strange mood. Who was I kidding? Nothing would ever change. I'd be stuck here in Missouri forever. I'd live under my parents' roof and go off to work in the morning just like I'd gone off to school every morning for the last twelve years, and in their eyes I'd always be a child.

When would I have a life of my own?

The next morning I walked into the dealership and Steve looked up and smiled at me like a cat that wanted to play with a mouse, and I was feeling more and more like the mouse. In spite of my pooh-poohing Jerome's fears, I knew his warnings weren't as ridiculous as I pretended they were. Steve was a lot older than I was. From the chat around the coffee pot in the service bay, I knew he'd been in the military, and it was easy to picture him with a gun, his finger on the trigger, those eyes gleaming like blue ice as he sighted his prey.

Stay away from me, I thought, and gave him a prim, tight-lipped smile. *Just mind your own business and stay out of mine.*

It was hard to ignore him. Whenever he walked in a room everyone would light up, eager to listen to whatever he had to say, grateful for any acknowledgment he might bestow. Everybody loved him or hated him, and it was hard to stay away from the magnetism of his personality because he was always the center of any group. He sold more RVs than anyone that first month.

Steve knew everything about the political drama of the scandals in Washington. The country was still reeling from Watergate and Nixon's downfall, and Steve always knew the latest breaking news. He made me feel so naïve. I felt tongue-tied around him because I didn't want to sound stupid. What did I have to contribute? I hated watching the news. I liked romance novels, stories about true love, or tales about women who overcame great obstacles to find their heart's desire. I spent my time trying to make sense of what he was talking about, or just trying to figure out a comeback for a jibe he took at me. The words that failed me during the day came to me while lying in bed at night. *If only he could have heard my comebacks then.* He rattled me like no one I had ever met!

Steve kept pictures of two beautiful blond children on his desk, and word got around the dealership that they were his kids, Stephanie and Stephen. Apparently he was separated from his wife Dorothy, who lived back in Michigan. They weren't legally divorced yet, but the papers had been drawn up and they were just waiting for the child support to be negotiated by the court and their lawyers.

One afternoon Steve and I crossed paths in a service bay at the back of the dealership—I had to go there to pick up some paperwork, and he needed to check out an RV he'd sold, to make sure it was clean before delivery. After I poured myself a cup of coffee, he walked over and helped himself to a cup.

Silently I poured some cream in my coffee and stirred it in while Steve looked me over with that knowing smile on his face, a smile I could feel in the pit of my belly. *Why couldn't I think of anything to say?* Everyone else who worked there could come up with a constant stream of polite chit-chat, but I couldn't even toss off a casual remark about the weather. The truth was, when Steve stood near me I had no idea whether it was raining or sunny. He filled up my senses until there was no room for anything else.

"You want some sugar with that coffee?" His voice was soft, teasing, and his gaze pinned me to the spot where I stood.

My heart raced with uncertainty, but I nodded shyly.

Slowly he leaned forward until his mouth pressed softly against mine. His lips were warm and moist, his skin smooth shaven with just a hint of razor stubble. I inhaled the scent of him and my knees buckled with desire as a bolt of electricity ran through me from my lips to my crotch and down to my toes.

Just the thought of that kiss makes me laugh out loud with pleasure. I was so shocked! Up until then I'd been completely infatuated with him, in spite of all his teasing, but I never dreamed he was attracted to me. I remember how nervous I felt. *What if someone saw us?* I still remember the smell of him, a clean, spicy blend of sandalwood and cedar that made me want to bury my nose in his neck and breathe that smell into my body.

It was over within seconds. Steve and I pulled ourselves apart and he smiled sweetly into my upturned face before he turned his back on me and went through the door to the showroom. I stood there in a state of shock, holding my coffee mug as if it might explode.

That one single kiss changed everything. I couldn't wait for each morning to arrive, because I knew I'd be going to work and seeing Steve. As the days passed by, we teased each other playfully and stole glances at each other when we had lunch a few times at Satan's Pit, the local barbeque—but we were never alone. We didn't tell anyone at the dealership about our flirtation, and no one seemed to suspect that we were attracted to each other.

Since Steve had just moved from Michigan to Missouri, he had no friends in the area, and one night in mid-November he asked me what I was doing after work. I told him that I was going over to my girlfriend Robin's house. He said, "Why don't you two come over and see my apartment?"

"Sure," I said. I was glad he gave me the option of bringing Robin. Even though Steve and I had shared that kiss, I would have been scared to go over to his place by myself. My only sexual experience had been with Jerome, and he was just a boy, even younger than I was. Steve was a good bit older than Jerome, and even though Jerome and I had parted ways by then, I wasn't sure I was ready to jump into a relationship with an older married man.

Of course my mother would have locked me in the house if she'd known where I was going, so I told her I was going to Robin's house and would stay there for the weekend.

Robin and I drove over in my car and Steve greeted us at

the door. His apartment was typical of the sprawling apartment complexes from that era, and when we walked in the door we were immediately in the living room, with the dining room and a very small kitchen attached to it. There was a tiny hallway with the bathroom off that, and a single bedroom in the back. A light tan shag rug covered the floor, and the apartment was filled with cheap rented furniture.

Steve offered Robin and me a couple of Harvey Wallbangers, a concoction he'd made with orange juice, vodka and Galliano. Three Wallbangers later, I was hardly able to walk. He drove Robin home, and when he came back and found me passed out on his bed, he gently removed my glasses from my face, folded them and placed them on his nightstand, then tucked me in his bed while he slept on the sofa.

In the middle of the night I woke up and tiptoed out to the sofa, drawn by a yearning I couldn't put into words. I couldn't help myself. I wanted to be near him. I wanted to hold him, melt into him, open my body to him and be held by him. Even though I was still hazy from the vodka, I knew what I wanted, and my skin was on fire with a longing I couldn't ignore.

The next morning I woke up in his bed, and the first thing I saw when I opened my eyes was the curve of Steve's naked back lying next to me. It felt natural to reach over and stroke his skin lightly with my fingertips, and he arched like a cat and purred at my touch.

"You took advantage of me last night," he mumbled sleepily. "There I was all tucked up on the couch minding my own business, and you came prancing out of the bedroom and popped the button of your jeans right in front of me."

"That's your story," I said. "I don't remember a thing." It was easy to talk to him when I couldn't see his face. I loved the smell and texture of his skin, and the sight of his beautifully muscled back. Sooner or later I'd have to get up and get dressed in front of him, and I worried about what he'd think of my body in the light of day. Compared to stick-thin models like Twiggy who dominated the fashion magazines of the day, I felt chunky.

"Harvey Wallbanger might have had a little to do with it." I could hear the smile in his voice, and I slapped him on the shoulder. He turned over and drew me into his arms, and I melted into him. No matter what happened to us, I knew that I'd begun the most important relationship of my life.

"You have the softest skin I've ever felt," he whispered. "Just like silk. Ah Penny, what are you doing to me? I don't want you to go. Why don't you stay for the weekend?"

I didn't think it over. I never gave a thought to my parents, or what might happen if they called Robin's house to check up on me. A deep unquenchable hunger for Steve made my answer seem inevitable. I was lost to the river of wanting him, and that river would pull me to whatever destination he chose.

"Yes," I whispered, and buried my face in his neck.

I stayed at his apartment for the weekend, and we made love everywhere: in the bedroom, on the floor, in the kitchen, in the living room, in the bathtub and standing in the shower. In the middle of one strenuous session, I started my monthly cycle. He had no qualms about going to a drug store to buy me tampons. He wasn't the least bit embarrassed by it and I loved his matter-of-fact acceptance of something that would have made most men blush.

I had never spent the night alone with a man, much less the whole weekend. I was completely naïve, but more than willing to learn. Steve only had to look at me before I felt the heat of his gaze flood my body with desire. He wanted me, and his wanting was enough to stoke the fire in me. We could not get enough of each other. Morning melted into afternoon, afternoon slid into evening, and we stayed in bed to touch each other again, and again and again. Making love became a world in itself, an exhausting, exhilarating, overwhelming need. We'd lift our heads to check the clock on the nightstand and laugh out loud at how much time had slipped away while we wrestled with each other between the sheets. For three days we didn't wear clothes. I was still shy enough to grab a towel to cover myself whenever I left the bed, but Steve walked naked to the kitchen to make toast and coffee before we slipped back to the urgency of our coupling. Whenever we tried to shake off the spell and get dressed, the smallest touch or word or gesture would set us off, and we'd fall into each other's arms once more.

Steve asked me how I'd ended up at the dealership, and I told him that I'd taken several business classes in high school, and wanted a career in business. When I'd graduated just five months earlier, I had a small scholarship, but I had no desire to go to college. For as long as I could remember, all I dreamed about was marrying somebody wonderful and having babies.

"You don't need kids of your own," Steve said. "Plenty of kids in the world already."

I drew back to look at him, surprised by his words. It never occurred to me before that I wouldn't have babies. It was the one certain thing I knew about my future. Steve would understand that, wouldn't he? "I want my own kids, though. At least two or three. My mom wants me to marry a doctor, move in next door and raise a family."

"Oh, don't do that," he said, and reached for me again.

"Stop," I giggled, and pushed him away. *Of course he'll give me babies*, I thought. *I'll make him come around.* "What about you? Where were you born? What's your family like?"

Steve sighed and reached for a cigarette and a book of matches from the night table. "Let's see." He placed a cigarette between his lips, scratched the match and touched the flame to the tobacco, then took a long sharp inhale and released a plume of smoke to the ceiling. "I was born in Manistee, Michigan. There were six of us—three boys, three girls. All of us but Larry were born in Michigan. Then my family moved to Connecticut, and Larry was born there."

I plucked the cigarette from his fingers. He made smoking look alluring and sexy, and I wanted to try it. The smoke burned my throat, but I loved the way it looked when it billowed out of my mouth. Steve watched me, clearly amused.

I stifled a cough. "What's your mom like?"

His face relaxed into a full, sweet smile. "She's crazy about me. Beaming proud of who I am, and ready to tell anybody about her son's amazing accomplishments."

"And your dad? Is he crazy about you too?"

He held out his hand, palm down, and tipped it this way and that. "We've had our differences. I left home when I was sixteen. I didn't want to move to Connecticut when the family moved, so I moved in with my uncle. Two years later I joined the army."

I gave him the cigarette and snuggled in close to his body.

"Did you go to Vietnam?"

"Nah. I was a surveyor, then a cook at Fort Riley, in Kansas. Man, I hated the military— they had way too many rules and regulations for my taste—so I did my two years and got out."

"How old are you, Steve?" I traced a circle through his chest hair while he took another drag.

"Old enough to know better." He released the smoke, stubbed out the cigarette in the ashtray on the night table, then turned to look at me. "I was born in 1940, Penny. So I'm … what, sixteen years older than you? Does that scare you?"

"No," I whispered.

There were pictures of his kids on the wall in the bedroom. They were gorgeous, like their father, about seven or eight years old. The sight of their cute blond heads filled me with a deep yearning.

"You ever think about having more kids?"

He gave me a sharp glance. "No."

I lowered my eyes and tossed him a seductive look. "You might change your mind."

His face grew serious. "I'm not having any more kids, Penny. I've had a vasectomy."

I was so young and sheltered, I'd never heard the word before. "What's a vasectomy?"

A smile twitched the corner of his mouth. "It means I've been snipped, darlin'. Doesn't affect the quality of the magic wand down there. It just means we can have a hell of a lot of sex without worrying about birth control, because I'll never make you pregnant."

His words stunned me. *How could I live without children of my own?* This was not the future I'd imagined for myself. In that moment I knew I had to get up and walk away from him forever, or else I'd have to give up every dream I ever had of being a mother.

He must have seen the dismay in my expression, because he abruptly changed the subject. "Did you grow up here, Penny?"

I covered myself with the sheet and pulled away from him slightly. My mind was still reeling from the shock of his announcement, and I struggled to act normal, to go on talking as if it didn't matter to me.

"I've been living in the same neighborhood practically my whole life. All the neighbors know each other, and have kids about the same age."

I can't leave, I thought. *I can't give him up.*

I forced myself to go on talking. "In the summer when I was growing up we all played hide-n-seek or kickball until dark."

"Sounds like *Leave it to Beaver*, Steve said.

"Sometimes. But my dad drinks. Not every day, but he goes on binges occasionally."

Steve lifted my arm and laid down a track of kisses from the inside of my wrist to the crook of my elbow. I softened under the gentle rain of his kisses. Whenever he touched me I melted and nothing else mattered. It was too late to pull away from him, too late to stop this feeling of wanting him, needing him in my life. I loved him. Every cell in my body knew it, and I was helpless to change how I felt. I loved Steve Milks.

Steve looked up from my arm, his blue eyes curious. "What about your mom? Does she drink?"

The thought of my mother made me feel guilty, and I wished Steve hadn't brought the image of her into bed with us. She didn't belong here. I was suddenly aware of my crotch pressed against the muscle of Steve's thigh, my bare breasts nestled against his chest.

I tried to give him a fair answer. "No, she doesn't drink. She has high expectations for all of us—him too, I guess—and sometimes it's hard for us to live up to her dreams for us. But she loves us like crazy. She always says her favorite feeling in the world is when she knows we're all tucked in bed and safe in our rooms."

As Steve and I lay in bed with our clothes tossed around the room, our bodies entwined and the sleepy Sunday sounds of a lawnmower buzzing down the block, somebody began pounding on the front door with enough force to rattle the windows.

"What the hell?" Steve muttered.

The pounding increased, and with growing horror I heard my mother's voice shout through the flimsy door. "Penny! Penny, are you in there?"

☙ Chapter Two ❧

"It's my mother!" I whispered.

We both leapt from the bed as if we'd been electrocuted. Steve yanked on a pair of pants while I pulled on my underwear, scrambled into my jeans, fastened my bra and buttoned my wrinkled blouse with trembling fingers.

The banging on the door never let up, and we could hear my mother shouting my name loud enough to wake the neighbors. "Penny! Penny, you open this door! I know you're in there! Penny! Do you hear me?"

If she kept up this racket someone was bound to call the police. Steve grabbed a T-shirt and pulled it over his head, then went to the front door in his bare feet. I tiptoed out to the living room and perched on the edge of a straight-backed chair, my body tense as a wire stretched to the breaking point. My palms started to sweat and I fought the urge to run or hide in the bathroom or jump out the window, anything to escape the scene I knew would erupt as soon as my mother came through that door.

Steve shot me one last look – a sort of visual shrug, resigned, apologetic and amused, all at the same time—then opened the door.

My mother blew past him and prowled the room, too angry to stand still. Her polyester slacks and blouse were freshly washed and pressed into blade-sharp pleats, in vivid contrast to the grimy clothes I wore. Even her hair seemed to bristle with outrage, and her rage sucked all the oxygen out of the room and burned hot enough to scorch anything or anyone in her path. I felt like a cornered rabbit.

Steve tucked his hands into his pockets and waited for her to settle down.

She gave me a withering glance, and then her eyes widened as she took in a pair of Steve's briefs dangling from the floor lamp next to the couch. Before she could open her mouth Steve crossed the room, snatched them up and stuffed them in his pocket, where they made an obscene bulge. He must have tossed them up in the air the last time he'd chased me around the living room and we ended up making love on the rug. I still had carpet burns on my buttocks from that episode, and my face heated up now just thinking about it.

"Is she pregnant?" she snarled at him. "Did you hurt her?"

"No!" Steve scoffed. "I would never do that."

Her eyes were wide with disbelief when she turned to me, and her voice softened as if we were alone together in the room. "Penny, why would you do this to your family? Did you think I wouldn't find out? Did you really believe you could disappear for three days—*three days!*—and that would be okay with us? We've been frantic!"

I stared sullenly at the floor. *How did she find me?* Now that she'd discovered my secret, what would she do? I'd never defied her before.

Although she was a petite woman—only five-foot-three in her stocking feet—she'd always loomed large in my mind. For as long as I could remember she seemed taller, more confident, and more certain of what was best for me. Like most mothers, she wanted me to live the life she wanted for me, and up until three days ago I thought I probably would. Now I knew the life she'd imagined for me was impossible. I didn't love the nice boy she wanted me to love, and I wasn't going to move in next door and give her lots of grandkids she could help raise. I knew she wanted me back in her nest, all tucked up in bed, under her roof, under her control and safe at home. What she didn't know was that I'd already left.

Her voice hardened, and her eyes threw sparks. "Did you hear me young lady? Go fetch your things. If I have to drag you out of here, I will."

I didn't move. After a weighted silence I glanced at the fierce expression on her face, brows knit, body tilted forward and hands white knuckled on her purse as she willed me to obey her.

We all knew she was there to save me from Steve, and it made no difference to her at all that I didn't want to be saved. I shrank into myself, crossed my arms tightly against my chest, put my head down and refused to meet her gaze.

Once upon a time I'd been the daughter who toddled into her kitchen and begged to lick the cake batter from the spoon. Ten years earlier I'd filled her living room with boxes of cookies to be distributed to each Girl Scout in my troop. I knew she wanted to go on being the mother of that girl. She wanted the Penny who played the clarinet and marched in the school band, the Penny who made the honor roll and won a scholarship, the daughter she could gladly point out to other parents and say "She's mine."

Her voice crackled with disbelief. "This just isn't like you, Penny. You were the one person in the world I thought I didn't have to worry about. I've always been so proud of you! I counted on you to make me proud." She stared down at me as if I were a stranger who had murdered her little girl, devoured her and replaced her with this eighteen year old woman who refused to obey her. Under that scathing glare I froze, unable to move or speak.

How could I explain to her how my life had changed in the past three days? I couldn't even explain it to myself. Granted, lust had a lot to do with it—every time Steve looked at me I could feel the heat between my legs—but there was a deeper pull as well. Everything that happened before I met him belonged to another world. Now I felt like Dorothy after her house crash-landed in Oz and the world turned from black and white to color. I wasn't in Kansas anymore. Whenever I turned to find Steve watching me with that sexy crooked smile, I felt alive.

Three days. That's all it took. He'd changed everything in just three days.

In the silence that stretched between us, Steve went into the kitchen, took a mug from the cupboard and filled it with wine instead of coffee. My mother had her back to him and didn't see him pour the wine into his mug, thank God, and I didn't say a word. He drained the cup in one long swallow, then refilled it.

Please, I thought. *You have to be strong enough to face her.* If he couldn't defend me now, I was lost. It made me afraid to see him drink as if he wanted to escape her. Did he want to escape from me too?

"Is it drugs, Penny? Are you both on drugs?" She picked up

a bottle of multivitamins from the living room table and shook the bottle until it rattled, then opened the cap and sniffed the contents suspiciously. "What did he give you?"

Steve walked back into the living room. "I would never take drugs, and I sure as hell wouldn't give drugs to your daughter." He lifted the cup to his mouth and took a big gulp.

"Her father will kill you," my mother said. "That's a promise. My God, how old are you anyway? You look like you're my age. Can't you see she's just a child? Look at her. Look at that face. She's a teenager! Is this the kind of man you are? Do you run around taking advantage of children? There are laws, Mister Milks. We'll call the police if we have to. You won't get away with it."

Steve raked his hair with one hand until it stood up in cowlicks all over his head. In spite of the tension in the room there was a familiar light in his eyes, a spark of interest. He loved a good debate, and so did my mother. Neither one of them was shy about wading into a fight, especially one that cut so close to home.

"Penny is eighteen," he said. "In the eyes of the law she's an adult. What about you? You must have started having kids when you weren't much older than she is now. Your parents didn't pick out your husband, did they?"

"What my parents did or didn't do is none of your business! You're a predator, and you're endangering my daughter's morals!"

Steve went on talking in a normal, everyday voice. "Didn't you make your own decision about who you wanted to be with? Would you deny Penny the same freedom?"

"This is fornication!" Mother yelled at him. "It's a sin against God!"

Steve rolled his eyes and went behind her back to the kitchen, where I saw him pour more wine into his cup. He caught my eye, pointed his forefinger to his temple with his thumb cocked upright to mime blowing his brains out. Then he lifted the cup to his mouth, gulped the wine down and poured another cupful. If she weren't here, he wouldn't be drinking like this. *Why didn't he tell her to leave?*

My mother scoured me with her gaze until I blushed, painfully aware of my bed-tousled hair, my unwashed face, and the smell of sex that clung to my skin. She shook her head as she studied me. I could see a vein throbbing in her neck, pulsing with her heartbeat.

When Steve walked back out to the living room she whipped around to face him, her voice raspy with frustration. "They told me at the dealership you have a daughter back in Michigan. How would you feel if some man twice your daughter's age took her away from you?"

Steve and I exchanged an uneasy look. If my mother had ranted to our boss about the two of us, we might not have jobs to go back to on Monday.

He shrugged. "When my daughter's eighteen, she'll be free to live with anybody she wants. I may not like it, but I hope I'll trust her enough to let her make her own decisions. And I might do exactly what you're doing now. But she'll be a grown up in the eyes of the law, and nothing I say or do will change that."

"Penny's a teenager!" my mother cried. "Do you know what it's like to raise a teenager? It's a full-time job. If you think she'll take care of you, do your cooking and cleaning, you should see her room! Clothes scattered wall to wall, books and records and makeup heaped up everywhere. You're taking on the responsibility for a child. Do you really want *another* child to raise, Mister Milks?"

"She's not a child," he said. "She's a woman, I'm a man, and we want to be together."

My mother stepped back from him as if she'd been shot. Two bright spots of red blazed in her cheeks, her breath shuddered, and her mouth opened and closed without making a sound.

Until this moment the woman who stood before me had always meant home to me. My mother had been my shelter, my protection, my guide to what was right and what was wrong. Until now she'd been the source of everything I knew, everything I was. Until this moment I'd loved her more than anyone else on earth.

But now my life had fused with Steve's life. His future was my future, and my destiny was his destiny. How did I know this? There are no good answers. I couldn't point to any rational excuse for the risks I took to be with him. I didn't really know him at all, but it felt as though my whole life had launched me to this point where our paths intersected and melted together. The love I felt for him seemed inevitable, unchangeable, a cloak of strength that gave me the courage to go on staring at the floor while my mother spit words at us like bullets, good old Baptist words like sin, damnation and hell fire, and we waited for her to run out of threats.

Her voice had run down to a whisper that raised the hair on

the back of my neck. "You'll burn in hell for this. This is evil. God will never forgive you."

"Leave her alone." Steve's voice was quiet, blurred from the wine he'd drunk, and he sounded almost sad, regretful that he had to say what needed to be said. "She's not hurting anyone. She's old enough to make up her own mind about who she wants to be with, and God doesn't have a damn thing to do with it."

Thank you, I thought.

Her eyes drilled me. "You're coming home with me, Penny. I will not let this man seduce you. Go get your purse. Get in the car."

"She's not going anywhere," Steve said. "She's with me now."

She ignored him, and kept her gaze locked on me. "Penny? Are you coming?"

I looked up at her and shook my head. "No."

She looked stunned, as if I'd kicked her in the chest. Her breath fluttered with short, rapid gasps, and I saw the shine of tears in her eyes as it dawned on her, at last, that I was really leaving her.

Her face twisted with raw, desperate sorrow as she continued to gaze at me. "Will you at least come to dinner tomorrow night? We'll all sit down and discuss this. Please. I'm begging you."

Steve shifted uneasily. "I have to leave for an RV show in Louisville. I won't be back until a week from Monday."

"Then we'll do it when you get back. Please. We'll have a civilized meal and talk this over."

Her pain was unbearable to watch, much worse than her anger. When she was angry I could hunch into a tight ball of resistance, but when her face crumbled into grief I had no defense. A lump formed in my throat, tears brimmed in my eyes and I glanced up at Steve and gave him a slight nod.

He let out a long sigh. "Fine. We'll come for dinner when I get back."

Immediately she straightened, as if she'd found a way to breach our defenses. She leveled her gaze at Steve as if she were sighting him through the crosshairs of a scope on a rifle. "A week from Monday, then. Six o'clock."

Silently I rose from the chair and opened the door.

She placed her palm on my arm and gave me one last searching look, then took a deep breath and walked out.

The next week I worked during the day at the dealership. Without Steve around, my job seemed mundane, repetitive and dull. The spark of sexual electricity that had made work seem like so much fun was no longer there. Now that he was gone, my life went back to black-and-white instead of Technicolor.

I stayed at his place at night while he was out of town for the RV show. I couldn't wait for him to return, and missed him terribly. The apartment was saturated with memories of our weekend together, but without Steve to give the place some life, I felt like I was camping out in a bar after closing time. No Steve, no sex, no drug of love or romance, nothing but ghosts. The bed was cold. The walls echoed with dull silence. The furniture couldn't talk to me. I was as lonely as I'd ever been in my life, and I couldn't—or wouldn't—go home.

Steve called me almost every night from the road, but his voice sounded distant, and I was too tongue-tied to think of anything interesting to say to hold him on the line more than a few minutes. Whenever my mother called I stonewalled her by keeping my replies to monosyllables. If she was going to act like I was a terrible sinner who was going to hell, then so be it. I wouldn't try to change her mind.

I bought two new polyester dresses so I'd have clothes for work. Each night I washed the dress I'd worn that day and hung it from the shower bar in Steve's bathroom so I could wear it again when it was dry. In the apartment I wore Steve's T-shirts and jeans, or his sweatshirts and sweat pants. He had a narrow butt, so his pants fit me well enough.

Every night I brought a burger, shake and fries from Hardee's and chewed the food in silence at the dining room table. I shoved all thoughts of home down in my belly, along with the fast food I could barely taste. I knew I had to make a clean break from my mother, or she'd never let me go. But it hurt to give up my family and not have Steve to help me bear it.

I kept the TV on all night to cut the solitude and the darkness.

In all the years we were together, this feeling of missing Steve never changed whenever he traveled. His absence in the bed always filled me with a sharp ache every time I rolled over and felt an empty cold spot instead of the warm bulk of his body. My life was always on hold until he came back.

Steve finally returned from Louisville late Friday night after I was asleep, and when he crawled into bed I stirred and held him tightly for a minute before he fell back against the pillows and dozed off.

As soon as I heard him start to snore, the tight and clenched feeling inside me relaxed a little, and all the misery I'd felt all week in this lonely bachelor pad swarmed up inside me like a nest of hornets. An overwhelming grief stung my heart as if it had been lurking in the shadows all week, waiting for me to let my guard down. Tears leaked out of the corners of my eyes and dripped into my ears.

I missed my family. *There.* The truth was out. As soon as I admitted it to myself, I felt the bitter despair of knowing that I couldn't have Steve if I chose them, and if I chose them I couldn't have Steve.

Was he really worth it? Was he really my soul mate, or was I fooling myself? In the black dark of that December night I asked myself if my mother might be right. Was this a terrible mistake? Was I throwing away a wonderful future with somebody else, somebody who could give me babies and a share a life with me? Somebody my parents wanted me to marry, someone who didn't make them crazy?

I could not afford to feel this way. It made no sense. I was just scared, acting like a teenager instead of the woman Steve thought I was. With an almost physical effort I stifled the sobs that threatened to rise up and burst out of me. I didn't want to wake him, and I didn't want to make him mad. My breath came in shallow, uneven gasps as I forced myself to swallow the tears. It took a long time for me to calm down. I counted backward from three hundred to zero four times in a row before I willed myself back to sleep.

A few hours later I woke up with a pain in my side that felt like I'd been stabbed. I could hardly get out of bed. I'd never felt anything like it, and the pain was so sharp—so impossible to ignore—it terrified me.

I didn't want to wake Steve. I didn't want to alarm him, and I didn't want to explain why I needed a doctor right away when I was doubled over and gasping with each breath. I knew he was exhausted from the drive back to Liberty. In my pain-addled brain, it seemed simpler to drive myself.

Without saying a word to Steve, I pulled on one of his clean T-shirts from the closet, slipped into my only pair of jeans and tiptoed out of the apartment to drive myself to our family doctor's office. As I look back on it now, I know it was a mistake to drive myself. Waves of cramps, nausea and pain washed through me like liquid fire, and I could feel beads of sweat pop out at my hairline as soon as I inserted the key in the ignition and started the engine.

I prayed the doctor would be there on a Saturday morning and see me without an appointment. Maybe he could give me a pill to calm the flames inside me. With one hand clutched to my side, I drove through the quiet streets of the neighborhood until I pulled up in front of the complex where our family doctor had his clinic.

By then the pain was so fierce I could hardly get out of the car. Each tiny movement made me gasp as I slid out of the driver's seat and lifted myself up by holding the door frame. It felt like I'd never be able to walk up the stairs to his office.

What is wrong with me? I wondered. *Am I dying?*

When the nurse saw me limp into the waiting room she rushed around her desk to meet me at the door. Her eyes widened in alarm as she took in my hunched figure, and I struggled to stay upright as I walked over to a chair in the waiting room. I wanted to sink to my knees on the carpet, crawl to a corner and curl into a fetal position.

"Penny! What on earth happened? Are you bleeding?"

I groaned, unable to answer because of the pain that clawed my belly.

She called out sharply for the doctor, who hurried into the waiting room and took me by the arm "Come on back to the exam room, Penny, let's settle you down on the table. Where does it hurt?"

"My left side. Ow!" I groaned as he helped me up on an exam table and lifted my legs to stretch me out full length.

The doctor stood over me, face stitched with concern, stethoscope slung around his neck. I could see the tufts of hairs in his nose, his eyes magnified by the thick lenses of his glasses. I'd never been in his office before without my mother.

"Does it hurt when I do this?" He pressed down on the lower left side of my belly.

"Yes! Ouch, don't do that."

"How about here?" he asked, moving his hands and pressing down again.

"Oh God, it all hurts." My head lolled to one side as I gasped in pain.

"Looks like it could be appendicitis, maybe gall bladder. Hard to tell. Either way, you'll need to check into the hospital for some tests. Blood work would show an elevated white blood cell count and let us know if we're dealing with an infection, or appendicitis, or gastroenteritis, or something else entirely." He patted my hand. "You stay right here and I'll call an ambulance."

"No!" I cried. If an ambulance came for me I'd really

feel like I was about to die, and that thought was too scary to contemplate. "I have a friend who will drive me."

"Then get him over here right now," the doctor said. "If it's your appendix, you don't have much time."

Steve was still asleep when I called him, but he woke up fast as soon as he heard the fear in my voice. Within ten minutes he appeared at the doctor's and whisked me away to the hospital, where I was checked in and scheduled for a round of tests for possible appendicitis or gallbladder problems.

For two days a team of doctors and nurses poked me and prodded me and argued among themselves over my symptoms, without ever coming to any conclusions.

On the third day Steve brought me a card from work, signed by everyone at the dealership. His face showed lines of worry and fatigue that I'd never seen in him before, and I reached out to draw him into the narrow hospital bed. He smiled, kicked off his shoes, got in bed and stretched out full length beside me while I covered us both with the sheet.

I nestled against the comforting warmth of his body. I'd missed him so much when he was in Louisville, and it felt stupid to be stuck here in the hospital now that he was finally back.

"Everybody's been worried sick about you, Miss P.," he whispered.

He smelled so good. I wanted to bank that smell in my memory, so I could pull it out and breathe it in whenever I was scared or alone. When I took in that scent, every muscle in my body relaxed.

"I feel better now," I said, and hugged him tight.

He put his arm under my head and snuggled against me.

"Your mom called me last night. She said the doctor wouldn't tell her what was going on with you. He said your record had to be kept confidential now that you're over eighteen."

I stirred against him. "I told her they didn't know what was wrong with me when she came to visit. What else did she say?"

He lifted a strand of my hair and smoothed it away from my face. "'Is Penny pregnant? Did she have a miscarriage? Did you give her a sexual disease?' She went on like that until I hung up on her."

"The doctors still don't know what happened," I said. "But I'm getting tired of hanging around here waiting for them to find out. I feel better now that you're here."

"Your dad called me last night. He was pretty far gone, sounded like he'd had one too many. Told me when he got through with me, the groundhog would be delivering my mail." Steve shifted uneasily. "Does he own a gun?"

I closed my eyes at the thought of the rifle in my dad's bedroom closet. He probably wouldn't hurt Steve, but I had no doubt my parents would do everything in their power to keep us apart. At the very least they could ruin Steve's reputation with their wild talk around town, and mine too. Who knows what else they might do if they were convinced it was in my best interests?

"What are we going to do, Steve?"

He put one arm behind his head and leaned back against the pillow to stare at the ceiling. "I've been thinking about moving back to Michigan. I miss my kids, Penny."

My heart nearly stopped. After all that we'd been through, after I'd pissed off my parents and let the stress of the past few weeks put me in the hospital, now—*now?*—he was going to leave me? My body turned to ice.

Steve went on talking as if nothing had happened. "Sooner or later I'll have to go back for the child support hearings. You think you might like to live in Michigan? My brother would probably be happy to have us move back into my old apartment up there."

Us. It was the sweetest word I'd ever heard. My arms and legs melted with relief, and I took a deep breath and let it go. I traced his profile as he lay on the pillow next to me, and lingered on his lips until he parted them and bit down gently on my finger.

"I've never been to Michigan," I said. "I've hardly been anywhere."

He turned to face me, lifted the hem of the hospital gown and slid his hand up the curve of my thigh. "Let's go, then."

"Yes." My legs opened to his touch, and the sweet warmth of arousal began to flow through me as his fingers dipped in and out, teasing, playing with the fire he'd started.

My mother called me at Steve's apartment as soon as she heard I'd been released from the hospital, and after a stilted conversation I finally agreed to bring Steve over for dinner the following night.

When I hung up the phone my stomach tightened into the same knot that sent me to the hospital a few days earlier. How could I sit through a family dinner at their house? They would never accept the fact that I was in love with a married man who was sixteen years older than I was, with two young kids of his own. It was hard enough to sit through the hour she'd spent yelling at us in his apartment, and if we met her on her own turf—with my father to back her up—it could only get worse.

Many years later my mother reminded me that her mom, my grandmother, had died the year before in 1973. My dad's mother—who had always been my mother's confidant—had breast cancer and was in the hospital about the same time that I was. She died the next year, in 1975. In retrospect I can see how those two deaths must have torn my parents up inside. It was probably the worst year of my mother's life, and I was about to make it even more painful for her.

The decision was easy. There would be no dinner. Instead, we made hasty plans for a clean getaway. I would withdraw the savings from my account, and then we would leave without telling anyone, not even our boss at the dealership or any of our friends. There was just one more thing I had to do before we left: sneak into my parents' house and pack for the trip.

The next day while my parents were both at work, Steve drove me over to their house. Wind shivered through the trees, and branches rattled like bones in the December wind. The sky overhead loomed battleship gray, heavy as iron, with clouds so low they seemed to sit on my shoulder. As we slowly edged our way toward the house I glanced nervously at the neighbors' windows to see if anyone was watching. With the coast clear, we parked and cautiously approached the house. When I heard Tammie practicing her scales on the piano in the downstairs rec room, I lifted my finger to my lips to signal Steve to remain silent.

I called down the stairs. "Hey, Tammie. It's me."

The ladder of notes halted. "Penny? What are you doing

here? Mom and Dad are still at work, and boy, are they ever mad at you!"

"I know. I just needed to pick up a few things. Go ahead and finish practicing—I'll be back later."

After a slight hesitation I could hear the notes continue, and I let out my breath in a sigh of relief. I gestured to Steve to go into the living room and wait for me. Feeling sheepish, as if I were a burglar in my own home, I tiptoed through the house, in a hurry to pack my things before my sister could realize what I was doing. There wasn't much time before she'd grow curious.

In the kitchen I pulled a brown paper bag out of the broom closet and filled it with the silverware and the New Pillsbury Cookbook I had bought for my hope chest. Next I tiptoed up the stairs and located my toothbrush and scooped up some underwear from my dresser. That was it—all my other clothes would remain crammed in the dresser or heaped in the closet. My skirts, dresses, slacks and jeans—my marching band uniform— everything I'd worn in high school now belonged to the shadow of my former self. I had no use for those clothes anymore.

Time to go. My father would be leaving work. I had to get out of there before his car pulled up in the driveway.

I paused in the kitchen and tore off a sheet of paper from the memo pad we kept near the phone. With trembling hands I managed to write out a note to my parents.

Dear Mother and Dad,

Sorry but we aren't staying for dinner. Steve and I are moving to Michigan. I promise I'll call you when we get there. Please don't worry about me.

Love, Penny

Tammie was still at the piano, dutifully plinking through a Chopin nocturne. She was just beginning tenth grade, and I wondered when I would see her again. On my way out I paused at the top of the stairs and called down to her. "I'll see you later, Toad."

To this day, I regret the way I left my family. If I could live my life over again and write a new beginning for me and Steve, this would be the first thing I would change about our story. I wish I had talked to Tammie and told her I was leaving. I wish I'd told her I loved her, and given her some reassurance that I would still be a part of her life.

Now that I'm older it hurts to think about the pain I caused my parents when I left Missouri. I wish I'd had the strength to talk to them in person, to tell them I was leaving, to ask them to trust me and to reassure them that I would be safe. They deserved that. I know my departure devastated them both, and I hope they can forgive me for it.

While I scribbled the note to my parents, Steve slipped out of the house to wait for me in the car. Finally I closed the front door behind me and carried the brown paper bag with my things out to the driveway, where he sat waiting for me in his Buick Riviera. Elbow slung out the window, the collar of his leather jacket flipped up, he gave me his big-bad-wolf smile and took a drag on his cigarette, then flicked it still burning on my parents' lawn. He was every mother's worst nightmare, and I didn't care. My guilt dissolved the moment I saw him grinning at me, and my heart expanded with happiness like a balloon filling with helium. In that instant I knew I'd follow him wherever he wanted to take me. From now on, Steve Milks would be my family.

I stowed the paper bag on the floor in the back, then jumped into the front seat, slammed the door and buckled my seat belt.

"You ready?" he asked.

I gave him a nervous smile. "Ready."

He revved the engine, pulled out of the driveway and roared up the street toward the highway. Mick Jagger's voice poured out of the radio, and I cranked the volume as high as it would go while we raced away from my childhood home.

I bet your mama was a tent show queen . . . Ah brown sugar . . .

✵ Chapter Three ✵

Every time I looked over at the handsome man behind the wheel, a sweet domestic thrill of belonging to him surged through me. He was the most gorgeous man I'd ever met, and he was my lover. Whenever I glanced over and saw him light up a cigarette or yawn or smile at a song on the radio, I thought *He is so cool.* I loved the way he moved, the way he talked, the way his tongue darted out to lick his lips when he was about to say something he knew would make me laugh. I loved the way he held the wheel of that Buick like he was master and commander of our world. Just the sight of him next to me on the wide leather seat of the car made me wiggle my toes in pure happiness.

Acres of snow-covered fields flowed by as the miles spun away under our wheels. The landscape was quilted with winter white, and it felt as though every living thing was asleep under the covering of snow. In the thin light of the December sunset, tree branches looked stark against the pale sky. Inside the car we sang along to the radio and laughed as we cracked pistachio nuts and tossed the shells on the floor.

Until then I had only been to three states, Kansas, Arkansas and Oklahoma, all within six hours of my home, and now I was on the road with the man I loved, burning up the miles and heading for new horizons. Our adventure together had begun.

With every mile we put between me and my hometown, the anxiety of the previous two weeks gradually slipped away. My mother's rage and disappointment in me flew out the window along with all my other worries. I was with Steve Milks now, and that was all the safety I needed.

Steve was excited about going home and seeing his brothers Larry and Buck, and of course he was eager to see his two kids, Stephanie and Stevie. Years earlier, Steve took Larry under his wing and straightened him out after Larry went through a phase of experimenting with drugs. In June, 1974, he married Marie. Larry and Steve had always been close, even though there was eleven years between them, and he'd told Steve we could move in with them until we found a place of our own. Larry and Marie were living in the same apartment that the three of them had shared before Steve left for Missouri, and most of Steve's furniture and belongings were still there.

According to Steve, Marie had the face of a china doll, and was trying to get some work as a model. Steve's brother Buck and his wife Edna lived six miles from Holt, and Steve told me we'd probably see them quite a bit too. All the brothers got along well unless alcohol was involved, and then Steve and Buck might use their fists to win an argument, while Larry and Steve just yelled at each other. Most of the time the brothers liked to hang out with each other.

Then there was Dorothy, Steve's wife. I felt nervous about meeting all these new people, but the thought of Dorothy made me more nervous than all of them put together. Steve said he was on good terms with her, and the only reason they weren't divorced yet was because the lawyers were wrangling over child support, but I knew I'd feel a lot better when those divorce papers were signed.

After we'd been driving for ten hours or so, darkness swallowed the view outside the window, and the only lights we saw were from cars and trucks coming toward us.

"Are we almost there?"

I'd asked Steve this question at least a thousand times, and he grinned when he heard it again. Since he knew the roads by heart, we didn't have a map in the car, so I had no way to track our progress. It drove me crazy not knowing where we were or how much farther we had to go. It seemed like we'd been driving forever.

"I'll buy you a road atlas, next time we stop," he said.

We left Missouri with a sock full of change from Steve's dresser and eighty-four dollars I'd taken from my savings account. After driving all night, Steve had run up a big bill on his gas card, and I'd spent almost all my money on snacks, meals and supplies for the road. It made me sad to see my savings evaporate in one long day and night of driving, and I had no idea how I'd ever save that much again.

With the Buick's big bench seats and extra leg room, we enjoyed a luxuriously comfortable ride, and the powerful V-8 engine could take us from zero to sixty in eight seconds. I loved the way I imagined we looked as we leaned back in our seats under the swooping boat-tailed roofline. The only problem was the Buick used up a gallon of gas every fourteen miles. Gas prices had zoomed from a quarter to fifty cents a gallon in the past year, and I was a little worried about how fast our money was disappearing. Inflation in 1974 was terrible, around fourteen percent, and everyone was worried about the way prices had skyrocketed. A typical home cost around thirty-five thousand dollars, and Steve said by the time he was ready to buy a house, one would probably cost fifty thousand. This seemed like an impossible amount of money back then, and I hoped he was wrong.

"Will your brother help you get a job?" I asked.

Steve gave me a look. "What makes you think I need his help?"

I folded my hands in my lap and twisted my thumbs together, around and around, letting them spin with the thoughts I'd been having for the last twenty miles or so. The more we drove, the more it cost. The more it cost, the more we needed to earn money. If we didn't earn money, we'd be stuck. Broke.

"We'll run out of money pretty soon. And you have to pay child support, right?"

Steve patted my hand in a patronizing "there, there" kind of way, as if I were a baby. "Don't you worry, Miss P. Larry will probably have a couple jobs lined up for me. I've worked with him before, installing house siding and carpet. He could probably use some help."

"I could work too." I'd already had two jobs. My first was at an arcade, where I'd fallen in love with pinball. I'd crank up the jukebox and listen to the Rolling Stones and play those pinball machines for hours.

Steve cracked a pistachio nut in his teeth and blew the shell on the floor. "You can work if you want, but there'll be plenty to do at home. One of us will have to look after the kids when they stay with us. Then there's all the washing, ironing, cooking, laundry, shopping and cleaning. If you want to take care of the kids and the house chores, I'll take care of the money."

I gave him a skeptical look. "You reckon installing carpet will support both of us?"

"Hell, I know how to do just about any type of work. I've dug septic tanks and pumped them, worked on the assembly line at Oldsmobile, even worked as a butcher. I'm not scared of hard work."

I settled back against the seat, slightly mollified. I kicked off my shoes and peeled off my socks and made faces at myself in the reflection of the dark window. It felt good to warm my toes in the blast of heat coming from the floor vent. Radio reception was too spotty to pick up anything but Christian stations here in the boondocks of Indiana, and I was still too shy around Steve to start singing on my own without the radio to back me up.

"Are we stopping soon? I need a rest room."

He yawned hugely, then blinked hard to keep his eyes open and checked the glow-in-the-dark numbers of the clock on the dash. "Okay. I have to release a few hostages myself. Keep your eyes peeled for a rest stop."

He checked the left lane, pulled out to pass a horse trailer and waited for it to signal the all-clear with its headlights before he tucked the Buick back into the right lane. We sped along between straight lines of highway stripes that disappeared beyond the cone of illumination cast by our headlights. A few fat flakes of snow slapped the windshield. It felt like we'd been in the steel cocoon of the car for days.

Steve turned on the wipers to clear away the snow that clung to the glass. "You see that? Michigan state line, dead ahead. We're getting close to home now. We'll stop up there."

At last we pulled off the interstate and slowed to a stop outside the visitor's center. After ten hours in the front seat, my body seemed to go on vibrating even after Steve turned off the engine. He opened his door, stepped out and shook one leg and then the other to get the blood moving again.

I handed him my wallet before he shut the door. "Buy me a map, okay? I'm going to the Ladies'."

The rest room was only fifty feet away, and a fresh blanket of snow covered the pavement between the car and the building. In those days I went barefoot whenever I could, and I didn't want to go to all the trouble of pulling on my socks and wedging my feet back into my shoes. I opened the door, jumped out of the car and sprinted for the bathroom.

A middle aged man with a long overcoat stood by the pay phone, and as I passed him his head whipped around as he stared in disbelief at my feet. I heard him say "There's a girl who just ran by me barefoot in the snow."

I felt so free. The snow was clean and cold under my feet, and I kicked up my heels like a colt as I raced toward the warmth and light of the visitor's center. In that moment my life seemed like a storybook stretching out ahead of me, with all the pages white and empty and waiting to be filled with beautiful pictures and no restrictions, no limits to what I might do. I was young enough and strong enough to do anything.

After I came out of the rest room and danced back to where Steve stood by the car, he grabbed me and lifted me into the air, laughing. "You crazy girl! It's so cold my dick looks like a button on a fur coat, and you're out here running around in your bare feet!"

I giggled and arched away from him as I struggled to get down. "Animals run around barefoot in the snow. Why shouldn't I?"

By now my feet were freezing, but I didn't care. He eased me back down and I sashayed around the Buick as if I were strolling through soft green grass instead of slush.

When we were both settled back in our seats inside the car, he tweaked my nose, his blue eyes sparkling with affection. "You know I'm crazy about you, don't you?"

"You better be," I said. "Or else I've made a terrible mistake."

Steve laughed out loud, and I glowed with the pleasure of hearing him say he cared about me. It made me feel so good. Up until then he hadn't actually said the words "I love you," but for him to say he was crazy about me was close enough.

We drove for fourteen hours, over I-70 East to St. Louis, Missouri, on to Indianapolis, Indiana, and up I-69 toward Lansing, Michigan. When we finally approached the city limits of Holt, southeast of Lansing, it was eight o'clock in the morning and my eyes felt sandy from being awake all night.

We entered a middle-class neighborhood on the outskirts of town and rolled to a stop in front of a duplex. Larry and Marie's apartment was silent in the early morning chill, and when we opened our car doors the air was cold enough to make me slide my feet into my socks and shoes before I stepped out of the car.

So this is Michigan, I thought. From the street the sidewalks and trees and houses looked a lot like Missouri, but it was a heck of a lot colder here.

We left our things in the car and walked to the door. Steve opened it, thrust his head in to call out to Larry and Marie, then ushered me inside.

The air inside the apartment was blissfully warm. It smelled like coffee. From the landing I could hear the sounds of a morning show on television in the room above us. We walked up half a dozen steps with a black wrought iron railing into the living room, and Larry and Marie jumped up from the couch to welcome us. After we'd all been introduced, Marie perched on a marble ledge in the picture window, and Larry and Steve and I stood there smiling awkwardly at each other.

"You help yourself to whatever you need," Larry said. "Your bed's all made up and waiting for you if you guys want to crash."

He was darker than Steve, younger, friendlier, and more eager to please. I liked him right away. Marie was pretty, with big brown eyes and a slender body. She had an otherworldly serenity, a gentle quality that I liked, and when she moved she seemed to float across the room.

Steve and I were so tired we were ready to drop where we stood, so we took Larry up on his offer and made our way down the hallway to the bedroom. It was the same bedroom Steve lived in before he left Michigan to work in Missouri. Good-sized compared to the bedroom I shared with Tammie back in Liberty, with a big four poster bed and a large dresser. A square window opened out to a view of dark fir trees and the back lawn of the apartment building next door.

We stripped off our clothes and climbed into bed, too tired

to do anything but collapse against the pillows. My body hummed over a phantom road, and continued to vibrate with adrenaline and nerves for quite some time. Steve fell asleep as soon as his head hit the pillow, but I stayed awake, staring at the acoustical tiles in the ceiling, listening to the unfamiliar creaks and groans of the apartment and inhaling the strange smells of Steve's bed linens. The pillowcase smelled like a woman's perfume, different from the Jade East cologne that Steve used. Had Marie come in here to take naps? I was acutely aware of being in an apartment that belonged to people I didn't know. It took me almost an hour to sink into a light doze.

"Get the fuck out of bed!" The voice was loud. Enraged. A woman's voice. She ripped the sheets and blankets off my body. I was stark naked under the covers. Dazed and terrified, I flailed around for a pillow to cover myself, then cowered behind it. Without my glasses I could only see her silhouette at the foot of the bed. Who was this lunatic?

Steve scrambled out of bed, his body tense. He was naked too, but he sounded like he didn't give a damn, he was going to kick some ass. "Goddamn it, Sue, what the hell do you think you're doing? Get out of here!"

Who the hell is Sue? I wondered.

She held the sheets and blankets clenched in her fists and shrieked at me in one long profane tirade. "You fucking bitch! I told you, get the fuck out of my bed! Fucking tramp, get up get up get UP!"

"Leave her alone! Shut the goddamned door and wait for me in the living room." Steve's voice was hard, loud and angry. I hadn't seen that side of him in the short time we'd been together, and his anger scared me almost as much as she did.

He grabbed his pants, pulled them on and blocked her view of me with his body, herding her out of the bedroom, through the hallway and down the stairs toward the front door.

I scrambled for the sheets and blankets she'd thrown on the floor and yanked them up until they were drawn up tight under my chin. I had a death grip on those sheets. If she was going to come back to the bedroom and try to rip the sheets off me again, I'd be ready to fight for them.

For a minute or two their voices were inaudible until I heard him shout "Sue, you and I are finished! You hear me? Do you? Because I swear to God, if I'm going to marry anyone, it will be that girl in my bed."

A door slammed, and Steve walked back in the bedroom, chuckling to himself.

My whole body was shaking, and I couldn't make it stop trembling. "Who was that?"

He peeled off his pants, climbed back in bed and snuggled close to me to warm his cold feet. "That was just Sue. Don't worry about it. Go back to sleep."

I lay there in bed thinking, *okay, that really helped*. We had never talked about his dating history, and beyond the fact that his ex-wife's name was Dorothy, I suddenly realized I knew nothing about him. He'd never even mentioned Sue. What if he had a more complicated history than he'd led me to believe?

For the rest of the day I barely slept. I felt myself startle awake every time I began to nod off, my body tense and alert to the smallest creak in the strange apartment, rigid with nerves whenever Steve shifted in bed next to me.

Finally I quit trying to go back to sleep, and left the bed to fix something to eat. Larry and Marie had already left, but they must have heard the commotion if they were still here when Sue arrived. I found some cereal and milk and poured myself a bowlful. As soon as I sat down to eat, Steve wandered out of the bedroom, looking sheepish.

I gave him a cool look over my Rice Krispies. "You want to tell me who Sue is?" I tried to sound casual, but my stomach was doing somersaults.

He shrugged. "She's an old girlfriend."

"How the heck did she get in?"

"Maybe Larry let her in. I don't know. She used to live with me, so she had a key to the apartment."

"But how did she even know you were here?"

"How the hell should I know? She probably saw the car."

"Did you get the key back?"

"Damn right I got the key back. That bitch. I left my checkbook with her when I left for Missouri, so she could pay my bills while I was gone. She started writing herself a few checks. I'm amazed she had the balls to show up here."

Jeeze Louise, I thought. *If that was his girlfriend, what will his wife be like?*

~

As luck would have it, I met the wife the very next day.

"Come on over," Steve said into the phone. "There's somebody I want you to meet. Bring your tweezers."

Dorothy arrived about an hour later, makeup kit in hand. She had long dark hair, a pretty face, and she began talking a blue streak as soon as she walked in the door. How was I feeling after that drive? Did I like to drive? Did I like Michigan? Was Missouri really different? What did I do down in Missouri? Had I graduated from high school? How did Steve and I meet each other? What pretty skin I had! Hers was problem skin, she told me, and that was why she had to keep herself creamed up.

As she rattled on I studied her, amazed to be talking to the woman who was still legally married to Steve, and even more amazed that she was so friendly. She had big breasts, and wore a tight top that clung to every curve, with skin-tight blue jeans. Her eyes were dark brown, almost black, and I thought Steve must like women with brown eyes, although Dorothy's were much darker than mine. Her skin was darker too, but very soft. Her makeup was flawlessly applied.

She laughed easily, and had an easy going personality. I felt more serious, watchful and shy, not nearly as light and breezy. And of course she was older— she was twenty-nine, just five years younger than Steve. At eighteen, I was younger than everybody.

Steve sat there staring at the two of us with that devilish grin on his face, as if he'd set us up to meet each other so he could watch the sparks fly. Who knows, maybe he wanted to show me off. That's what I'd like to think. But the look on his face said he'd enjoy himself no matter what happened.

"Look at those eyebrows." He tilted his head toward me.

Dorothy's river of chit-chat came to an abrupt stop. She came closer to where I was sitting on the marble ledge of the window and peered intently at my face. "Oh, good Lord. I see what you mean. They're a little woolly, aren't they? But what a gorgeous face. Look at those eyes! Penny, you're going to look like a new woman when I get through with you."

Steve stood, walked over and leaned in toward my face until their two heads filled my field of vision. "Think you can wrestle those caterpillars into submission?"

Dorothy studied me with a compassionate look on her face. "What do you say, honey? You want to look like Liz Taylor?"

It had never occurred to me that my eyebrows were wild, or that Steve didn't like them. I was shocked. What was wrong with them?

Dorothy must have seen the confusion on my face, because she leaned in close and gently removed my glasses from my face. "Just give me half an hour and you'll thank me, I promise. You're going to look like a movie star when these are pruned back a little."

I thought *this is how things are now*. This was my new life, after all, in a new place, with a new man. Why wouldn't my face become a different face?

Shyly I nodded consent, and as soon as I did, Steve walked back to his chair with a little swagger, as if he'd won a point.

I watched Dorothy set out tissues, Q-tips, a bottle of alcohol, tweezers and a tube of antiseptic ointment. I'd hardly said two words since she arrived, but words kept flowing out of her and easing the skittishness out of me.

"Now this might make you sneeze, or it might make you cry. You just let me know if you need a break, and we'll stop. Have you ever tweezed before?"

"No, ma'am."

"Now don't you give me any of that ma'am business, you're

going to make me feel like an old lady. Tell me, what do you do for fun down there in Missouri, aside from fooling around with my husband?" She gave me a broad wink and shot a grin at Steve, who burst out laughing. My face heated up, but with both of them smiling at me I had to smile too.

Over the next hour she tweezed my eyebrows slowly and carefully, and she gave me a thousand beauty tips about how to maintain my skin and hair and what makeup to wear. Her breath smelled sweet, like bubble gum, or fruit-flavored toothpaste. It was comforting to hold my face up to her and feel her work her way slowly and methodically over my brows. Even the sting of each hair being plucked out by its root gave me a sense of accomplishment, as if I were one step closer to being the girl Steve wanted.

"Why did you two get divorced?" I asked.

Steve's eyes twinkled as the silence developed between Dorothy and him. I felt like I'd thrown a ticking bomb into the middle of the living room, and they were trying to outwait each other to see who would get stuck with defusing it.

Silence went against Dorothy's nature. Finally she let out a sigh and rolled her eyes, her tweezers poised over my skin. "I was way too young when I met him. Only sixteen. He was twenty-one, he should have known better."

"We had Stephanie and little Steve," Steve said. "It was all worth it." He yawned and stretched both arms up and over his head, then eased himself back in his chair. It crossed my mind that he might be bored because we weren't scratching each other's eyes out. But the truth was, I liked Dorothy.

"Well sure it was worth it, when you put it that way. But I

was totally overwhelmed by marriage and motherhood, and we were miserable because we were living with my parents."

Steve smiled at the memory. "When Stevie was two she told me to move out and take my boat with me."

"That's right. He moved up the street into a hotel."

"I was working for her dad, but he fired me a month later. Gave me a severance check. I was so mad I ripped it up in front of him."

"Idiot," Dorothy murmured under her breath. "You should have given it to me. I could have used that money."

"Do you have a boyfriend?" I wasn't too worried about Steve going back to her, but I really hoped she had a boyfriend.

"Mm-hmm." She tilted her head and studied me for a moment. "Once I moved out of my parents' house and had an apartment of my own, I met Jim."

Steve hitched himself out of the chair and walked down the hall, and a moment later we heard the toilet flush. He didn't come back to the living room, and I wondered if the thought of Jim still upset him.

Dorothy shook her head slowly, lost in her own private reverie, and when she spoke again her voice was lower, as if she didn't want him to hear. "We put poor Jim through hell, because Steve and I were on and off with each other for the next five years. It took me a long time to realize Jim is the man I want to be with. So I filed divorce papers, and Steve left for Missouri. Good thing, huh? That's how he met you." She let out a conspiratorial giggle and gave me such a warm look that I couldn't help but laugh too.

Life was so strange! Here was this woman, talking and

laughing as if she was my new best friend. Maybe it didn't matter that she was still married to the man I loved, the man I'd risked everything to keep, the man I'd staked my life on. Maybe Dorothy and I had more in common than her husband. And maybe that was okay.

She dabbed my sore pinpricked skin with a Q-tip soaked in alcohol, delicately applied the antiseptic salve, then sat back to survey her work as she eyed me critically. "There! How are you holding up? Your skin will be red for a day or so, and those follicles might scab up on you, but after a week the skin around your brows will go back to being smooth and beautiful."

She took a small hand mirror from her makeup bag and offered it to me so I could see my new face. I took the mirror and stared at the two elegantly trimmed brunette chevrons that gave me a slightly surprised look and gracefully framed my brown eyes. I could hardly believe the change.

"Thank you," I said. I meant it. I reached out and took her by the hand, and she looked so touched by that simple gesture that I jumped up and hugged her.

She whispered in my ear. "Penny, you are exactly what Steve needs. I can tell he's crazy in love with you. When do you want to come over and meet the kids?"

❧ Chapter Four ❧

What if his children hate me? I thought. *How much loyalty can I expect?* Steve had never even said the words "I love you" to me, so what would he do if his kids couldn't stand me? Would he get rid of me if they pressured him to cut me loose? In the list of his affections, who came first?

Even Steve seemed a little nervous when the time came to pick them up from Dorothy's for our first weekend together. He was always immaculately groomed, but on that Saturday morning he spent a long time showering and shaving and combing his hair. He wore his favorite pair of jeans and a crisp white shirt I'd only seen him wear at work.

I wore blue jeans and a turtleneck so tight it strangled me, but it was the nicest shirt I could find to wear in the limited wardrobe I had.

"You think Stephanie and Stevie will like me?" I asked.

Steve inspected his sideburns in the mirror, turning this way and that, and drew the comb over the left sideburn in tiny strokes to make the hair lie down flat. "I think they'll be glad they don't have to put up with Sue anymore. She was no good with the kids."

I pondered that for a while, and wondered if that was why Steve dumped her. What did it mean to him, to be *good with kids?* More and more I felt like I was about to walk onstage without knowing my lines, to audition for a role I had no idea how to play.

"What exactly did you do with them on the weekends they stayed with you?"

"Watch sports on TV, mostly. If I went out to the bar, Sue or Marie would look after them."

I didn't say anything, but raised an eyebrow at him in the mirror. Sue might not have been good with kids, but it didn't sound like he was going to win any father-of-the-year award.

The comb paused in mid-air as he caught my reflection in the mirror. "Why? What are you getting at?"

"Doesn't sound like much fun, that's all."

Steve snorted. "You think I should sit around playing baby games with them? Dorothy does plenty of that. If they want to be around me, they know things will be different at my house. They have to fit into my life."

For the first time I wondered if it might be a good thing for his kids to have me in their lives. They must have been bored out of their minds at Steve's apartment if he didn't play with them. Me, on the other hand, I loved kids, and I loved playing all kinds of games. When Tammie was little we used to play Monopoly, Sorry, Operation or Candyland for hours, and if we were outside we'd go ice skating or sledding or have snowball fights. I felt a little lift to my spirits at the thought that I might play those games again.

I sat on the lid of the commode, polished the lenses of my glasses on my shirt and slid them back on my nose. "Maybe we could do a little more for them."

He put his comb under the tap and let the water run over

it, then slicked it through his hair one more time. "You mean take them out to dinner? Go to the movies? There's no money for that."

He moved closer to the mirror to check his sideburns. "I'll tell you what I do for those kids: I pay for every bite of food they eat. I pay for every roll of toilet paper, every bar of soap, every single tube of toothpaste they use. I take them to the candy store every time I drive them back to their mother's, let them buy any damned thing they want, just so they'll have something sweet to remember about their visit with me. I pay for the roof over their heads, and I pay for every Christmas present they get."

His voice dropped to a mutter, grumbling to himself now. "I don't see why some fat man in a red suit gets all the credit, because I'm the only Santa Claus those kids will ever have."

I rolled my eyes and held up my hand to make the "talk, talk, talk" gesture, thumb and fingers clapping together like a duck's beak.

Steve was absorbed in his reflection, so he didn't see it. He re-tucked his shirt into his waistband, gave himself one more look in the mirror, then winked at me. "Come on, Miss P. Let's do this thing."

Stephanie and Stevie raced across Dorothy's living room to hurl themselves into their daddy's arms. He might not have been the best father in the world, but there was no doubt about it: those kids loved their dad. Steve swept them up in a big bear hug and let them hang off his neck and his waist while Stephanie gave me a suspicious, narrow-eyed once over, and Stevie leaned against his father's leg, too shy to look me in the eye.

They're so young, I thought. Only seven and eight years old. Both had Dorothy's black-dark brown eyes and Steve's blonde hair. Stephanie was petite and slim, with broad shoulders like her father, and she held herself erect, with the poise of an older child. No frilly girl clothes for her—she wore corduroy pants, a long sleeved T-shirt and white snow boots. She stared at me with barely concealed hostility, her thin little arms crossed over her chest, distrust radiating from every pore. I knew she'd be ready for a fight if I tried to boss her around.

Stevie was smaller, a little chunkier and quieter than his big sister, but he looked hopeful when he finally met my eyes and managed to smile. He wore a striped T-shirt, corduroy jeans and blue snow boots. His face was so open and innocent it made my heart ache.

I wanted to gather them both up in my arms and say *you can relax. You're safe. Things will be better now.* I stood perfectly still and held my breath, as if I were trying to approach two wild fawns.

"This is Penny." Steve stood and gave them a gentle push in my direction. "She's with me now."

I let out the breath I'd been holding. *There. At least that part is over.*

Doubt lingered on Stephanie's face, while Stevie stuck out his hand for me to shake. I crouched down on one knee, shook his hand and grinned up at him.

"Glad to meet you, Stevie. Did Santa put any presents for you under that tree?"

"I got one from grandma," he whispered. He zoomed over to a small Christmas tree that occupied a corner of the living room, grabbed one of the wrapped packages underneath it and brought the box over for my inspection.

Underwear, Dorothy mouthed at me, and ruffled his hair. "Santa won't come until Christmas Eve, right Stevie?"

"Right," he said, and hugged his present to his chest.

The shoelace on his right sneaker was untied, so I tied it for him, happy to have something simple to do to calm my nerves. He leaned against me while I made the laces snug and tight. I loved the warmth of his hand on my shoulder, the sturdiness of his little boy legs, the shampoo and bubble gum smell of him. When I finished tying the laces and reached out to pat his cheek, his skin felt soft as a kitten.

Steve coughed. "We better get a move on, kids. The Raiders are playing this afternoon, and kick-off is in ten minutes."

The light in their eyes disappeared, as though he'd thrown a switch and shut off the power behind their smiles. They gathered their coats with slow, heavy movements, like mourners getting ready to go to a funeral.

Dorothy let out a sigh of exasperation. "You haven't seen these kids in a month! You expect them to sit in that damned apartment with nothing to do while you watch a football game on TV?"

"There's plenty to do," Steve said. "They could learn about sports. They could do their homework. They can do whatever they want."

I looked at the snow falling thick and fast against the windowpanes. Already a foot of snow had collected on the ground, and another few inches were due to arrive overnight.

I took Stevie's hand in mine. "I've been waiting for a chance to build a snowman ever since I moved up here, but I might need some help. This is Michigan snow, and it's fluffier than Missouri snow. If you know anybody who could teach me how to make a snowman, I could use some advice."

Stevie glanced up at me, his eyes alert. "I know how to make a snowman."

I squatted down until we were face to face. "You think we could have hot chocolate after we get done? I could make hot chocolate with little marshmallows. You like it with marshmallows, or without?"

Stevie looked up at his mother, who nodded encouragingly. "I like marshmallows."

I smiled at him. "Maybe after dinner we could write a letter to Santa Claus so he knows exactly what we want for Christmas. You want to write him a letter?"

Little Stevie beamed at me, then burst into a series of very large hops around the room, apparently so excited by the thought of snowmen, hot chocolate and Santa Claus that he looked like he might blow a gasket.

Stephanie gave me a hard look, as if she knew it was only a matter of time before my dark side would emerge. I could see the tug of war going on behind her eyes, but I could tell she was tempted to join in the conversation.

I looked up at her. "After that, who knows? We could play cards. Do you know how to play slapjack?"

"Yeah, I know how to play slapjack." Her eyes remained guarded, watchful, tough as a prison warden, but at least she was talking to me.

Steve and Dorothy exchanged an amused glance. "Okay, let's hit it," he said. "Last one to the car is gonna have to run alongside us."

"I get the front!" Stephanie yelled, and raced out the door.

It was ridiculous, I knew, but when I followed her out and saw her climb into the front seat of the Riviera I felt a pang of jealousy. *She's in my seat,* I thought. Yes, she was only eight years old, and I was an adult, a full ten years older. But it was hard not to feel like I might have to compete with her for Steve's affection.

Steve gave me a smile that said *you wanted kids, right? Here they are.*

That weekend I had more fun than I ever expected to, while Steve made his nest on the couch and watched football on TV. The kids and I raced around and nearly trampled him to death as we played games of chase, tag and tickle monster. The kids tested me the way puppies will gnaw on you until you show them you're the boss, but I never quite figured out how to convince them I was the boss and make them obey me. I felt more like their sister than a parent figure, and only Steve could tame them when they got too wild. Steve grumbled about the commotion, but we could always get him to laugh during the commercials, and a few times he joined us in the fun. The kids and I pelted each other with popcorn and marshmallows, sang the jingles to the ads we liked and built a fort in the bedroom. We played outside in the snow and I laughed so hard I felt like I'd done a thousand sit-ups by the time Monday rolled around.

On our way back to Dorothy's we took them to the candy store, a dark and dingy place that was a kid's paradise inside, lined with shelves full of candy bars, gum, licorice, Twizzlers, maple nut goodies, Mary Janes, any kind of candy you could want.

There was a big cooler full of ice cream bars and Eskimo pies.

Steve told the kids they could have as much candy as they could carry to the counter at one time. Stephanie loaded her arms with every kind of chocolate candy bar, while Stevie carried a mound of Bubble-icious bubble gum and a stack of Heath bars. Steve and I bought a pile of Bit o' Honeys for ourselves.

For days afterward, the taste of honey would remind me of our kids.

It amazed me how much my life had changed in a few weeks. One day I was just another teenager fresh out of high school, and the next I was crossing state lines with a thirty-four year old married man, playing step-mom to his two kids and shacking up with him a thousand miles away from my childhood home.

I was a little shell-shocked by the suddenness of it. I'd hardly ever had a drink in my life, and now I was drinking beer or wine or hard liquor every night. I wasn't used to making love two or three times a day, either. My body felt raw from having sex all the time, and even though I was head over heels in love with Steve, I was exhausted.

After we'd been in Michigan for a week or so, Steve called his family in Connecticut to tell them we would be there for Christmas.

We drove for fourteen long hours through the dreary winter darkness of the northeast. It seemed like night fell at about three-thirty in the afternoon, and even when the sun was up the sky never became really light. It remained a dim gray, the color of twilight, the color of lead.

As the miles drained by, each fence post and telephone pole

reminded me that I was going another thousand miles away from my family in Missouri. This would be the first Christmas I'd ever spent away from home, and the thought gave me a fierce ache in my chest. Would Mother and Dad ever forgive me for running away? Would Tammie hate me for abandoning her? Every time I heard Johnny Mathis sing "I'll Be Home for Christmas" on the radio, I felt like an orphan.

Finally we arrived at Steve's parents' house, a small three bedroom ranch house on Norman Road in the town of Lebanon, Connecticut. As soon as we stepped inside the front door, Steve's mom folded me into her arms. Ma was a tiny, chunky woman, no more than four feet ten inches tall in her stocking feet, with breasts as big as pillows. When I hugged her I felt something prick my chest, and pulled away to see what had stabbed me. There were about a dozen safety pins fastened to her smock, and one of them had sprung open and nipped me.

She chuckled when she saw me staring at the pins. "I like to keep a few of these around in case someone needs one."

His father jumped up from his Lazy Boy recliner as soon as we walked in the house. He wore a baseball hat pushed back on his head at a rakish angle and had the pale complexion of a Northerner, flecked with scars from a car wreck he'd survived when he was a young man. He peered at me from behind his tortoiseshell glasses and gave me a brisk hello. "Penny, is it? You graduate from high school yet?"

"Yes sir." I shot a nervous look at Steve, and he grinned. I suspected that he enjoyed being seen with someone so young. If Dorothy was only sixteen when he married her, it wasn't too hard to figure out that he liked young women.

Steve kissed the top of his mother's head. "Ma, you look great."

"Did you have a good trip? How's the Buick running?"

"It's been squeaking a little, the last few miles. You wouldn't happen to have an extra fan belt in the back room, would you?"

"You know I think I picked up an extra belt for you after you bought the Riviera last year. I bet I could find it for you if you give me a minute. Come in and make yourselves at home. Penny, you are the cutest little girl I ever saw! Can I help with the suitcases? No? You look like you're half frozen, you poor child—your nose is as red as Rudolph's. Are you hungry? No?"

As she walked past me I could see the pockets in her smock were stuffed to bursting with candy bars, crackers, peanuts and snacks.

She was the ultimate packrat.

We stowed our gear in one of the bedrooms before Ma led us on a tour of the house and proudly showed off a bedroom she'd converted to storage. It was a sight to behold, stacked to the ceiling with boxes, newspapers, clothes, dressers, chairs, lamps, magazines, tools, birdcages, scrapbooks, bolts of cloth, blankets and pillows. The door didn't open all the way, and there was barely enough room to walk into it.

The bedroom Ma and Pop shared was cram-packed to the ceiling with stuff, with a narrow aisle surrounding the bed and pathways to the dressers. There were about six dressers in there, and later on I discovered that most of the drawers were filled to bursting with old newspaper clippings, magazines, books, puzzles, games and all kinds of junk, her treasures, she couldn't throw away.

Steve's mother disappeared for a long time and finally emerged from her bedroom with a brand new fan belt for the Riviera clutched in her fist. You could ask her for anything in the world and she would disappear into the back and come out with it an hour later.

Steve and I cleared a space for ourselves in the living room, and we spent most of the next ten days camped out on the couch in front of the TV while Pop dozed in the recliner next to us. Pop worked the night shift at Pratt and Whitney Aircraft, while Ma worked at Colt Firearms during the day.

On Friday night his dad tried to get him to go out drinking at the local bar. They'd always gone out and partied together in the past, but now that I was in the picture, Steve wouldn't budge. Steve could see I was feeling homesick, and it worried him.

Ma went out of her way to make me feel welcome and loved. She sensed that I was homesick, and pampered me whenever she was around. This mothering made me feel relaxed enough to tell her anything.

When I met Steve's sisters, though, it was a different story. They terrified me. They were loud, confident, strong women, and I was so shy and scared I couldn't think of anything to say to them. I worried that they might think I was a snob or—even worse—a dumb redneck.

"How you like it up here in the frozen north?" one of them asked me.

I paused too long while I thought *I hate it here, that's how I like it. I'm homesick and miserable and I have no idea how to be clever like you.*

"Fine," I whispered, then cleared my throat and said it again, too loud.

My fear of saying something stupid led to long uncomfortable silences where I knew I should say something, but I couldn't come up with anything, and as the minutes ticked away the silence only became more uncomfortable.

I began to crumble under the pity that radiated from them. They could see I was tongue-tied, and they knew I was homesick. I huddled on that old couch in the living room and kept my eyes glued to the TV. It felt like I had to tuck myself into a tiny ball to remain invisible or I might break down altogether.

My thoughts became darker and darker. The fact that Steve had never told me he loved me preyed on my mind, and I fretted over the way he never quite looked me in the eye when I told him I loved him. He said he was crazy about me, but maybe he just meant he was crazy, period.

Why was I here? What had become of my life, my home, my family? Yes, I loved Steve, but it was hard to give up everything and everyone else I loved, especially at Christmas. By now my mother would have the stockings with our names stitched across the tops tacked up to the mantelpiece. Those stockings were a big deal in my house, and I hated to miss out on them. The week before Christmas Mother wrapped presents at the dining room table, and I loved the heaps of wrapping paper, bows, boxes and ribbon that spilled onto the chairs. I loved the way our house filled with a wonderful molasses and sugar fragrance of gingerbread men baking in the oven. I could almost see Tammie laying out her allowance money in piles on her bedspread to figure out how much to spend on each person in the family. Dad would play "I Saw Mommy Kissing Santa Claus" and scoop up my mom for a waltz around the living room. To miss all these things felt like a little death inside me.

I called them on Christmas day. Not just to wish them merry Christmas—I missed them terribly.

"Penny, are you sure you're all right?" my mom said as soon as she heard my voice. "I miss you so much, baby. When are you coming home?"

Tears sprang to my eyes, and I started to cry. "I can't come home, Mother."

"Of course you can! It's Christmas, honey. You don't want to be away from your family on Christmas! Give me your address, and I'll come and get you."

"You can't. I'm at Steve's parents' house in Connecticut. They've been real good to me."

She heard the tears in my voice, and her voice became so soft it broke my heart. "But they're not your family, Penny."

"You don't understand! I'm with Steve now. He is my family."

"Oh Penny, it's not the same, he's not—."

"We're married, Mother." The lie popped out of me before I could pull it back.

"Married?"

"We went to a justice of the peace on our way to Connecticut." *Shit!* The lie kept spinning out of me, and it turned the silence between us into an icy black hole.

"You're married."

The disbelief in her voice spurred me on. "I told you, I'm Mrs. Steve Milks now."

"Are you pregnant?"

There was a coiled tension in her question that alarmed me, as if she might grab the shotgun in my dad's closet and head for Connecticut to blow Steve into the afterlife if he'd knocked up her baby girl.

"No! I can't get pregnant. He had a vasectomy back when he was married."

"A vasectomy!" There was a stunned pause. "So the two of you won't ever have children?"

"No." My throat hurt with unshed tears. "No, Mother, we won't have children."

"Oh, Penny." Her voice was so soft, so miserable, I couldn't bear it. After a long pause I heard the muffled sound of her crying. I closed my eyes and held the receiver to my forehead. *What was I doing? How could I have made everything even worse?*

"Mother, I have to go." I knew I'd burst into big racking sobs if I stayed on the line one more second. "I'm happy, okay? I hope you can be happy for me too."

I put the receiver back on the hook and sank to the floor, my head buried in my hands, filled with a misery so deep and hard I knew it would last a lifetime.

It scared Steve to see me cry. I couldn't snap out of it. We spooned on the couch in the living room and watched endless games of football on TV while the tears dripped down my cheeks and I dabbed my eyes with a handkerchief. Up until now we'd had a sweet honeymoon, nothing but good times, lots of sex, smiles and laughter, but the honeymoon was over. I was a wreck. He had no idea how to help me go back to being the cheerful Miss P. he'd fallen for in the first place.

I was a long way from the girl who ran through the snow in her bare feet.

One night we overheard his father grumbling to his mother in the kitchen. "What's wrong with him? Usually I can count on that boy to come out to the bar and have a few drinks with me when the holidays come around. Now all he wants to do is stay at home and hold hands with that little girl."

"It's about time," Ma snapped. "I think Penny is the best thing that ever happened to him."

"That girl put a spell on him," Pop said. "It's not natural."

Pop's disbelief at the change in Steve rattled my notion of who Steve really was. If Pop thought his son was a carefree bachelor who drank all night and slept with cocktail waitresses every chance he got, what made me believe that Steve was the love of my life? What if I was no more than a fling to him?

"Come on," Steve whispered in my ear. "I'm going to take you out. We'll have a few drinks, make the old man happy, and maybe it'll brighten your spirits."

An hour later we were sitting in a bar called the Log Cabin, and after I'd had two shots of vodka with orange juice, tears welled up and began to pour down my face. I took off my glasses and wiped them, then put them back on. They immediately fogged up again. I felt ashamed of myself, but I couldn't make myself stop.

"Steve, I'm so homesick," I whispered.

I slumped over and buried my face in his shoulder. I felt sick from the alcohol, from the puzzled looks his father kept giving me, from the way his sisters shook their heads and glanced pityingly at me. I couldn't believe I'd lied to my mother and told her I was married. I'd always been so honest, and honesty was important to me. *Who was I, now that I'd run away from home?*

I was sick from the effort to fit in, to not make waves, to be good and pretty and nice when every cell in my body felt stretched to the breaking point by this terrible homesickness. I wanted my mother. I wanted to lie in my old bed once again. I wanted our family Christmas tree, our stockings, our songs and jokes and games. I wanted my family back. I couldn't stand feeling this way. I just wanted to go home.

Steve kept his eyes fixed on the blue TV screen above the bar. "Shh, baby. You'll feel better tomorrow."

I pulled away from him and cradled my head in my hands. "No. I won't feel better tomorrow, Steve. I'm miserable. I miss my family. Nothing here belongs to me. These aren't my people. I feel like a stranger."

He sighed, obviously fed up with my depression. "It's just Christmas, P. Lots of people get depressed at Christmas. You've been listening to too many of these lonesome songs they're playing on the jukebox."

A hiccup rose up in me and turned into a sob. "Steve, please. I want to go home."

He closed his eyes briefly, then opened them and stared at me. He knocked back his shot of whiskey in one long pull and clapped the glass down on the table. "Okay."

I sat back. "Really?"

He kept his eyes fixed on the empty shot glass.

"You'll take me back to Missouri?"

He looked at me and shook his head. "I can't deal with these crying jags any more. It's not good for either of us. You need to make a choice, and then stick to it. We can't go through this every time you get homesick. If you want to stay, stay. If you want to go home, I'll take you there."

For some reason his words made me even more miserable. "I guess you can't wait to get rid of me, huh."

He kissed the top of my head, then lifted my chin to kiss me full on the lips. It was the softest kiss I'd ever felt, even softer than the first kiss he'd given me back in Missouri. There was yearning in it, and something like sorrow.

I was the first one to pull away.

His eyes were so sad. He lifted a lock of my hair away from my face and twirled it around his finger. There was no sly smile, no laughter in his expression. He studied me as if he wanted to tattoo my features on his memory, and he let his gaze linger a long time on my eyes, my mouth, my hair. He let the strands of my hair trickle through his fingers until he'd released them all.

"I don't want you to leave. If it were up to me, you'd never leave. But I can't stand to see you hurting like this, honey. You tell me what you need me to do. I'll drive you home, if that's what you want. I just want you to be happy."

Everything he said made me feel worse. "I feel so stupid. You'd probably be happier with someone older. Someone more mature."

"Not a chance," he said softly. "You're the only woman in the world for me. Don't you know that? There's nobody else who could come close to making me feel this way. I love you, Penny Long. I'm crazy in love with you."

My heart did a little dance in my chest, and the vodka rushed through me in a blaze of light.

I love you, Penny Long. I'm crazy in love with you.

His words fizzed through me like champagne, like fireworks, like happiness itself, and laughter rose up inside me and spilled out. *He loves me.*

I grabbed his neck and hugged him so hard he started to choke, and then I kissed him all over his face while laughter and tears continued to bubble out of me.

"Does this mean you're leaving me?" he asked, wincing under the onslaught of kisses.

"Never," I told him.

❧ Chapter Five ❧

When Steve and I returned to Michigan, Larry told us the lease on the apartment was about to expire, so in January of 1975 we moved along with Larry and Marie to a one bedroom apartment on Aurelius Road in Mason, about five miles away from Holt. We made the apartment into two bedrooms by putting up a curtain on the back half of the living room. That half of the living room was our bedroom.

Even without privacy, Steve and I were blissfully happy. Our sex life flourished, and it wasn't unusual to make love two or three times a day. We took advantage of every moment alone and sometimes moments we weren't alone. The challenge of finding those precious hours when we could be by ourselves only stoked the fire of our longing for each other.

One night we drove off in the Riviera to a dirt road outside town that had become our favorite lovers' lane. We made love in the back seat of the car with the windows rolled down, accompanied by a chorus of spring peepers in the woods around us. While we rested afterwards Steve spent a long time nibbling, sucking and licking the skin across the top of my chest. It was a pleasant sensation, like being suckled by a kitten, and I could feel a warm tingle between my thighs as he moved inch by inch in a slow circle below my neck. After several minutes he lifted his head to gaze at his handiwork, then looked up at me with a lazy smile, his eyes heavy-lidded with satisfaction.

When I glanced down I saw he'd given me a necklace of pink hickeys.

He circled my nipple with his thumb, and I could feel him hard against my leg, swelling with a bottomless lust that matched my own. "Want to do it again?"

"Yes," I whispered, and sank once more into his arms.

I loved living with him. While he went job hunting I did all the laundry, ironed his dress shirts, picked up his kids whether Steve was home or not, and helped Marie with the cooking and cleaning.

Life was wonderful, except for one thing: we had no money. Our savings were almost gone.

In June Steve faced a court hearing for failure to pay child support. This wasn't because Dorothy brought a complaint—she received money from Steve whenever he had it—but the court insisted that the child support payments had to be officially assessed and enforced. Steve and Dorothy had filed papers for divorce, but the divorce hadn't become finalized.

When Steve finally went to court, the judge set his child support payments at fifty dollars weekly. He also had to pay back support, which would come out of future paychecks.

Steve did his best to convince the judge this was unreasonable, especially since he had no job. Fifty dollars a week seemed like an impossible amount of money to pay Dorothy when we were just scraping by.

The judge suggested Steve sell the Buick Riviera.

Steve cursed under his breath at that idea, and the judge

eyed him coldly, ready to cite him for contempt.

Needless to say, we did not sell the car.

A week later Steve had an interview with Champion Home Builders. The vice-president of the recreational vehicle division drove to Charlotte, met with Steve and was so impressed he hired him on the spot. At long last, Steve would have a good salary, and Champion would reimburse him for his expenses as he traveled through the Eastern and Southern territories as a salesman of Class C mini-homes. These cute little RV's had most of the amenities of a larger motor home, but had better gas mileage, since they were smaller and lighter.

Steve was thrilled by the job offer. I should have felt happy for him—it was a great opportunity—but I was secretly terrified of living without him while he went on the road for Champion. By now I was completely addicted to this man and the warmth of his arms around me as I went to sleep each night.

The night he was hired, we talked in whispers behind the curtain that separated our bed from the living room. From the other end of the apartment we could hear Larry and Marie move back and forth from the bathroom to the bedroom. Water gurgled through the pipes, then cranked off. The muffled sound of their conversation floated into our half of the living room as we lay back against the pillows with Steve's arm around my shoulder. It was a hot July night, and there was a film of sweat on our bodies after the long sweet tussle of our lovemaking.

How will I fill all the empty hours without him? I bit my thumbnail, thinking about that question.

"I'll need a new suit." The low rumble of Steve's voice vibrated through my body, and he stretched his arms overhead like he was emperor of the universe. "A few more dress shirts, slacks, maybe even new shoes. You want to sell RV's, you can't look shabby."

He smells so good. I inhaled his scent deep into my lungs to store it in my memory for the lonely nights ahead, then traced the line of hairs that pointed down to his navel.

He arched under my hand until I tickled his pubic hair, using the light touch he loved.

"I hate the thought of you leaving me alone here," I whispered.

He stirred under my fingers. "Come on, Peeps, I have to work. How else are we going to afford a place of our own? Don't you want a place we don't have to share with Larry and Marie?"

"You know I do. It's just hard to imagine being here without you. How often do you think you'll be able to come home?"

He turned and kissed the tip of my nose. "The travel won't last long. You watch. I'll move up in the company, and then I'll be home so much you'll get sick of me."

I held my tongue, although I had a sinking feeling that without Steve, my life would go back to black and white instead of Technicolor. No more long rides out country lanes where we could park and look up at the stars and tell each other the story of our lives. No more sultry nights filled with the slick hot tangle of our bodies as they melted into each other.

My mind went back to the ultimatum he'd given me in Connecticut. If I couldn't learn how to be strong and put on a happy face, he'd take me back to my parents' house. At this point there was no way I could go home to Missouri and pretend to be a child after he'd made me feel like a woman.

Suck it up, I thought. *What choice do I have?*

In June of 1975, Larry and Marie moved to a different apartment, and this time they didn't ask us to move with them. They were ready to be on their own. Steve and I wanted a place of our own too, but there was no way we could afford the rent on an apartment by ourselves.

Even though he was making good money with Champion, we were still hard pressed to catch up, financially. It was tough to save an extra fifty dollars a week for child support when we had to make payments on the Riviera, buy gasoline and shell out cash for food, clothing and rent.

Steve was terrible with money. It slipped through his fingers like water, and I hated to see those dollars disappear into tips, loans to friends or impulsive gifts for me or his family. He never balanced his checkbook, and we were never sure exactly how much was in the bank.

To save money, Steve convinced me that we should move into his older brother's rundown farmhouse. Buck and Steve got along fine as long as they weren't drinking, and Steve wouldn't need to sleep there more than once a month, because he'd be on the road. Buck's rent on the farmhouse was $85 a month, and Steve offered to give him that much if we moved in. It was a lot cheaper than any apartment we could find.

Buck was three years older than Steve, and his wife Edna was ten years older than Buck and had five kids before Buck married her. Then they had two children of their own, so the farmhouse was already cram-packed with kids and grown-ups when Steve and I moved in.

Earlier in the year Buck had been laid off from Diamond Reo, a heavy truck manufacturer in Lansing that had gone bankrupt. He was taking unemployment and living on food stamps when we moved in with them, and they also had some government assistance for two of their kids, who were mentally disabled.

The first time I saw the interior of their farmhouse I thought, *Oh my God, what have I just walked into?*

The place was a shambles. I peered up at the living room ceiling, which had fallen down in places to reveal a lattice of joists that supported the roof. Buckets half full of dirty rainwater sat under the leaks to catch the water. The rooms were tiny, with no doors, just arched openings between them. One small bathroom contained a sink and tub stained with rusty water and many years of use. The kitchen linoleum was old and torn, and a room off from the kitchen had a dirt floor. No insulation in the walls, floors or ceilings, and the only heat came from a smelly fuel oil heater.

When Steve and I walked in we saw Buck and Edna at the kitchen table, chain smoking non-filtered Camels and drinking beer. Empty bottles of Pabst Blue Ribbon littered the surface of the table. The ashtray smoldered from half a dozen butts that were still going, and the air was thick with smoke and the odor of stale beer.

When Buck saw us he leaned back in his chair and said "Steve! How the fuck are you?" Edna gave me a wry smile, her eyes like slits against the smoke that curled up from the cigarette hanging from the corner of her mouth. Buck wore a clean

T-shirt and jeans and had a big round beer belly, while Edna wore a blue chenille bathrobe that had seen better days. I could hear "The Price Is Right" blaring from the TV set in the living room.

"Come on in, Penny, don't be shy," Buck said. "We cleared the kids out of the bedroom down here, so you can park your shit in there." He pointed toward one of the main floor bedrooms, a cubbyhole with no door, just an arched opening to the living room.

"Thanks," I said weakly.

"You hungry? There's a pot of chili on the stove, it's probably still hot."

"No, sir, I'm fine."

"Sir!" He turned to Edna. "You hear that? Makes a nice change from *old fart*."

Edna let out a smoker's laugh that sounded like a handful of rocks thrown in a blender. "Don't get used to it."

Steve nudged me forward. "Go on, sit down, make yourself at home."

I perched on the edge of one of the kitchen chairs and gave them a tight smile. *I will survive,* I told myself. *I might be miserable for a while, but I will get through this.*

Voices from the upstairs rose in a crescendo of shrieks until we heard the thud of something being thrown against the wall. The whole house echoed with the impact, and I flinched at the curses that poured from the kids upstairs.

"There's our girl." Edna peered through the smoke at a young woman who slowly descended the stairs.

"Hi," I said softly. The girl's wild, matted hair, slack expression and the dark circles under her eyes let me know this was one of their mentally disabled kids.

She stopped in her tracks, her gaze fixed on me, then slowly retreated back up the stairs, her tongue working against her lips.

More and more, I had the sinking feeling that I was moving into a horror movie.

This was nothing like the apartment we'd shared with Larry and Marie. Marie and I had always made sure our place was spotless, windows washed, floors mopped and waxed, and all the appliances were new. It seemed like a mansion compared to this place, and I clutched Steve's hand in panic at the thought of living here without him while he traveled.

How will I stay sane? I thought. There was no sanctuary here, no silence, no clean, orderly space where I could shut the door and be quiet and think my own thoughts.

Dorothy had already told us in no uncertain terms that she didn't want Steph and Stevie to come over here, and I didn't blame her a bit. In Buck's house, every other word was "fuck" or "shit," and Buck had an endless supply of dirty jokes. The kids were neglected and feral as wild animals, and with all of us crammed into that house there was a palpable tension under the surface of every conversation.

I knew Steve couldn't wait to get out of there. As soon as he finished packing for his next sales trip, he said goodbye to Buck and Edna, and then the two of us walked out to the driveway for a private farewell. The sun had already set, but a pale glow remained in the sky, and the first stars were just beginning to show.

Champion had given him a new mini-home to drive from city to city, and I desperately wanted to jump in that cozy little vehicle and go with him.

Even though I put on a bright smile for his sake, I couldn't help but cling to him. He had been my whole world for the past eight months, and the thought of letting him go off without me for three weeks was almost more than I could bear. The silhouette of the farmhouse loomed over us like a malevolent ghost, and I hated the thought of going back in there alone.

"Come on, baby, don't worry." He hugged me and patted my back, but I could feel him lift his wrist to check his watch. "Next time I go out on the road I'll see if you can come with me."

My hands tightened on his back. "You promise?"

"Promise. You be good, okay? If Buck starts drinking, you steer clear. Let him sleep it off." He pulled himself away from me and fished three twenties out of his wallet. "Here's a little gas money for the Riviera. Buck borrowed it today, so he has the keys. You want to go anywhere, you just tell him."

"I'll miss you," I said forlornly.

"I'll call you every night. Come on, Peeps, let go now."

Steve gave me one last kiss, then stepped briskly to the door of the mini-home and jumped up in the driver's seat. A few seconds later the engine roared to life, and I knew he was thrilled to ride off on a grand adventure in a brand new vehicle, ready to meet new people and see new places.

I stood there in the driveway watching until his tail lights disappeared, and then the darkness enclosed me.

For the next three weeks I tried to fit in, smile a lot, keep my mouth shut and fill the empty hours by reading Harlequin romance novels. Sometimes I worked problems in a college entry exam book I bought to help me remember everything I'd learned in high school, but most of the time I felt like I was living in purgatory. Steve called every day, sometimes twice a day, and it felt like my life revolved around those phone calls.

During the two and a half months I lived at Buck and Edna's I always felt like I had to ask Buck for permission to drive the Riviera. Buck used it several times a week to go to the horse track, which was a little over an hour away. The Riviera was much more reliable transportation than the junker they owned, and Buck kept the keys to the Riviera in his hip pocket.

Stuck at home with Edna, I spent hours listening to her complain about their financial situation. She knew that whenever Steve came home for a visit, he gave me a little bit to see me through the month. Within a day or so after he left, Edna would make me feel so guilty that I'd hand the money over to her for groceries. She always seemed to think we owed her, and I had no resistance when she hinted that I should give her more.

"Here it is Monday," she said, squinting through the smoke from her Camel, "and we've been out of milk for the kids for two days now."

"I had about a half a cup on my Rice Krispies yesterday," I admitted. I knew what was coming, and I hated it.

"Government check won't come 'til Friday." She gave me a long hard look. "Don't know when we'll have the money to get some more milk."

Then why does Buck always have money to bet on the horses? I wondered.

"Kids need milk." She stubbed out her cigarette in the

smoldering ashtray. "You should know that, you want to be a step-mom."

I pushed my chair back from the kitchen table and stood up. "I'll get my wallet."

Most of the time I tried to hold my tongue and listen to them without judging them, but it was hard. Even though they were good people at heart, my nerves were scraped raw by the end of each day, and I longed for the moment when Steve and I could move into a home of our own.

When Steve finally returned, he kept his word and took me out on his next road trip for Champion. We called on RV dealers in Ohio, New York, Connecticut, Kentucky, Virginia, North Carolina, Georgia and Florida, places I had never seen before, places that filled my heart with beauty and hope.

Every day felt like a honeymoon. A friend of Steve's gave us a Chihuahua puppy we named Candy, and she went with us on the trip. She loved the road life as much as I did, and traveling with Steve thrilled me. I loved the horse farms in Kentucky with the white picket fences around the fields, houses and even the trees. I had never seen the ocean before, and when we crossed the causeway bridge in St. Petersburg, the sight of the vast blue expanse of the Gulf of Mexico took my breath away. The autumn foliage in the Blue Ridge Mountains burned with color that remains seared into my memory to this day.

After a couple weeks on the road, we finally made our way back to Michigan and ended up back where we started, sitting in the driveway at Buck's, both of us reluctant to get out.

The sky was flooded with the dark reds and purples of the

dying sun, bathing the farmhouse in the color of blood. I stared at the sway backed roof and dreaded the reunion that was waiting for us inside.

Steve pulled the keys from the ignition and shifted slightly to push them into his hip pocket. "I have some hard news to tell you."

A cold lump of fear weighed on my chest, and my hand tightened on the door handle. "Just say it, whatever it is. Spit it out."

He sighed. "You're not going to like it."

Every muscle in my body tensed, and I clutched the door handle as if my life depended on it, but I let the silence remain.

He stared out the window. "I can't take you with me on the road anymore."

All the air left my body, and the bright hopeful feeling I'd begun to feel out on the highways suddenly collapsed. "Why not?"

"My boss wants me to travel with the reps he hired last week. I'm supposed to teach them the ropes. Plus he wants me to work more RV shows."

I felt like an orphan, lost in the silence that followed this announcement, my heart swamped with self-pity when I thought about how much I'd given up to run off with Steve. Now I wasn't even going to be able to live with him.

I turned my face away. "You're making good money now. Can't we find a place of our own?"

"Not yet, Peeps. I'm still behind on the child support. We have to wait a little while longer."

"So I'm stuck here." I stared at Buck and Edna's farmhouse

and felt the adrenaline kick of a panic attack gather inside me, crouched and ready to seize me by the throat.

One morning I asked Buck for the car keys and he shook his head mournfully, looking at me with his big puppy-dog brown eyes as if it broke his heart to turn me down.

"Can't do it. There's a guy I have to meet at the track this afternoon."

Up until now, he'd never dared to say "no" when I asked for the keys. He might bitch and moan about it, but he'd never refused outright.

"No problem," I said, and held out my hand. "I'll be back by noon."

He gave me a suspicious look. "What the hell are you so fired up about?"

Escape was so close I could almost taste it, and I knew I'd feel a hundred pounds lighter as soon as I pried the car keys away from Buck. "You'll see. It's a surprise. You'll like it."

He snorted in disbelief, but finally dug his hand in his jeans, fished out the keys to the Riviera and passed them over to me.

I nearly flew out the door of that ramshackle farmhouse, jumped in the Riviera and zoomed down the driveway fast enough to make the gravel spit under my tires.

During our phone conversation the night before, Steve finally relented and told me I could begin looking for a place of our own. That morning I launched myself into the search with the desperation of a prisoner who sees a ladder propped against the jailhouse wall.

As soon as I walked into the duplex on Dell Road, I knew

this was the place for us. The houses on the street were widely spaced and the back yard extended to a chicken coop and a cornfield in the distance that belonged to the owner of the duplex. The house had a bright, clean look to it, with plenty of green grass and a country setting. Everything inside looked new: new windows, carpet, walls, plumbing, toilet, stove and refrigerator. No leaks in the ceiling, no torn up linoleum, no dirt floors and best of all, doors on every bedroom.

Spacious rooms with white walls and a light green shag carpet opened out to big windows that overlooked the back yard. A finished basement contained two bedrooms with rust colored shag carpet, and there was even a utility room for the washer and dryer we might buy some day.

The rent was $235 a month plus utilities. A big jump from the $85 we paid Buck each month, but I knew we could manage if we were careful.

For three long days I waited for Steve to arrive, and when he finally showed up at the farmhouse I rushed him over to Dell Road so he could see the place for himself.

I hovered at his elbow and pointed out how wonderful it would be to have all this space for the kids to play, not to mention a brand new kitchen where I could learn to cook great meals. Steph and Stevie would have their own bedrooms downstairs, while the master bedroom on the main floor would give us all plenty of privacy.

"Well?" I asked.

"It's expensive." He was too cool to show much emotion, but I could see from the gleam in his eye that he liked it.

Nestling my head against his shoulder, I snaked an arm

around his waist and squeezed. "I'll figure out the money. We'll sit down and chart all our monthly expenses, set aside what we need for the kids, the car, the rent and utilities. We can swing it if we're careful."

He tilted his head to press his cheek against my hair. "I'd need a credit card, just to skate over the next couple months. Not that I have a chance in hell of getting one."

Hope made my heart start to gallop. "I'll take care of it. I'll go down to the bank and talk to the manager."

Steve let out a bitter laugh. "Don't get your hopes up, Peeps. My credit's no good. With this child support mess, they'll turn you down flat."

I wanted this so badly I willed him to see the future I saw, to believe in the life I envisioned for us. *We belong here,* I thought. *This is the beginning of our happily ever after.*

I looked him in the eye, on fire with determination. "They won't turn me down. You watch. I'll promise with all my heart to pay them every month if they give us a credit card with a $300 limit. We can do it, Steve. I know we can. If we're never late, we'll build up our limit."

I squirmed away from him and began to walk around the empty living room, too excited to stand still. "Once we establish credit with the bank, we'll go to Sears! You like that Johnny Miller collection, don't you? We'll open a revolving credit card account with them and get you a couple of new suits."

He leaned against the living room wall, hip cocked, hands in his pocket, a half-smile tugging at the corner of his mouth. "I never saw anybody get so excited about revolving credit."

"Steve, if you let me handle our finances I swear we'll save money. You know you never balance your checkbook, and you hate to write checks and pay bills. Why not let me do it? I promise you'll always know how much money you have, right to the penny."

He smiled that lazy sexy grin of his, blue eyes twinkling. "You really want this place?"

I stopped and stood there looking at him, my heart beating against my ribs like a bird fluttering against a wire cage. "Yes. Yes I do."

He nodded slowly and took one final look around. "All right then. Let's do it."

For a split second I froze, staring hard at his expression to make sure he meant it. Then I swept him into an embrace, kissing him all over his face until he began to laugh out loud.

I paused in mid-kiss. "I'll make sure we can afford it, Steve. I promise I'll figure out the money. If we make a budget and stick to it, by this time next year we'll be ready to buy furniture."

His gaze never left my face, and when he spoke his voice was full of love. "You really think you can handle high finance?"

"Try me," I said, and kissed him again.

When we returned to the farmhouse, Steve and I sat down at the kitchen table with Buck and Edna, and I told them we were going to move.

Buck looked at me like he thought I was nuts. "Why rent another apartment when you can stay here with family? You have a place to sleep, food on the table—it's practically free! You won't find a deal like this anywhere else. What more do you want?"

I glanced anxiously at Steve. These were all the reasons that

Steve had given me when we moved in with Buck, and they were still true.

Steve caught the look on my face, squared his shoulders, pushed his chair back and stood up from the table. "It's high time Penny and I had a place of our own."

Buck looked up at Steve and gave him a crooked smile, a hint of sorrow in his eyes. "How long you been at Champion? Three, four months? Last year I thought I had a job too, but then I got the call saying Diamond Reo is bankrupt. This economy, Champion could go under next week. Then what? You'll be up shit creek, that's what. In debt and out on your fuckin' ass."

Steve stood there in silence for a few seconds, taking in Buck's full measure, his eyes calm, his gaze steady. At long last he held out his hand to me, and I took it.

"We'll take our chances, Buck." He drew me to my feet, and I stood so close to him it felt like we were one body, one soul. "Come on, Miss P. Let's pack it up."

On our way to our first night in the duplex, we stopped at K-Mart and bought an inflatable air mattress to use as a sofa, then went to Kentucky Fried Chicken for a bucket of chicken and biscuits.

We sat on the carpet in the living room and ate right out of the bucket, and when the last biscuit had been buttered and eaten, Steve licked my fingers one by one, and I licked his.

He gave me a look I knew well. "You ready to baptize this carpet?"

There were no curtains on the windows, and anyone who walked up to the house could look in and see us. "What if our neighbors stop by to say hello?"

He moved closer, lifted the hem of my T-shirt and slid his palm over my belly, taking his time, leaving an electrified tingle in my skin. "We'll say 'Please come back some other time, because I'm busy fucking my darling.' "

My heart beat glad and strong as a drum, so loud I was sure he could hear it.

With one finger he tilted my chin up, then leaned down to kiss me. His lips were warm, his breath sweet, and as he pulled me close a flash of heat spread through my limbs, a yearning that felt as deep as gravity, drawing me toward him.

Taking his time, he reached behind me, lifted my shirt and slowly coaxed it up above my breasts, pulling it higher until I had to raise my arms to let him ease the T-shirt past my chin and over my head. He tossed the shirt on the floor, then bent down to untie my sneakers. Kneeling in front of me, he unzipped my jeans and tugged them down, and I stepped out of them. My skin prickled into goose bumps.

He drew me down to the carpet and let his fingers brush the satin cups of my brassiere, teasing me with a slow back-and-forth stroke. "I've missed you, babe."

All the restraint I'd felt for the past three months buckled and collapsed, as if I'd been hiding for a long time inside walls that were toppling now. It was wonderful to be crushed against his chest, to feel the rough warmth of his face pressed against mine and smell the rich salty tang of his sweat. My skin felt electric, shimmering everywhere that he touched me, and my legs began to tremble.

"I want you," I whispered.

"I'm right here." His lips almost touched my ear, and I could feel his breath on my cheek.

After we made love I floated from room to room in a state of euphoria, opened and closed all the doors and traced the walls and windows with my fingers.

The empty rooms thrilled me. No more Buck and Edna, no more Larry and Marie, and no more parents telling me what to do. No more smiling and nodding and catering to everyone else when it came to the space around me. For the first time in my life I would live in a place I could decorate myself, and have a kitchen where I would make all the decisions about what meals to cook. No one would come into this apartment unless we invited them. I could read, or study, or play the clarinet, or walk around naked if I wanted to, or spend all day on the air mattress, watching the clouds roll by outside my window. This was the sanctuary I'd longed for. This was home.

My fingers caressed the new Formica counters in the kitchen, the knob for the water faucet and the shiny outline of the stainless steel sink. I touched the handles on the kitchen cabinets, the light switches, the refrigerator and stove. I opened the empty drawers and imagined filling them with dishes and silver and potholders and cookbooks. As I drifted from room to room I kept touching everything with a little smile I couldn't wipe off my face, and my throat swelled with happiness so pure and intense it filled my eyes with tears.

Mine, I thought, and *Ours.*

❧ *Chapter Six* ❧

On the morning of September 7, 1976, the light from our bedroom window bathed us in a soft buttery glow that made the room shine with possibility. It was my twentieth birthday. I closed my eyes and made a birthday wish, then opened them and traced the halo of light that shimmered over the line of Steve's wrist, up his arm to his shoulder and the side of his face. In that end-of-summer light his hair looked like white fire. After three long weeks without him while he traveled on the road for Champion, I loved waking up in his arms. I loved his face. I loved his body. I loved his smile, the way he moved and the way he talked. I loved everything about the man who lay snoring beside me in the rumpled sheets.

We'd been living on Dell Road for over a year, and it had been almost two years since I'd run away from Missouri to live with Steve. The duplex had turned into a cozy little nest for us, and at long last, I was the ultimate happy homemaker. Dorothy gave us a coffee table and an old television, which Steve said he'd bought in the first place, so she was just giving it back. I found a table with four chairs marked down at K-mart and a neighbor gave us a double mattress and box springs. After a year of saving, we asked Larry to co-sign for us at Bob De Loach Furniture so we could put a down payment on a living room set.

Sometimes I'd catch Steve with a funny little smile on his face as he watched me move furniture around, then stand back with my fists on my hips to survey the results. I knew he got a kick out of how thrilled I was to have a place of our own. He'd already had lots of apartments, so ours was nothing new for him, but for me it was the first time I was in charge of furnishing and decorating a home.

I loved everything about living with him, except for the crushing loneliness I felt when he walked out the door to go back on the road. Nothing was enough to combat that desolate feeling of standing in the driveway with tears filling my eyes as he drove away and left me behind.

I could have found a job, but after nearly two years away from my last one I felt too shy to go looking for work. I'd spent a long time tucking myself into Steve's shadow, especially when we lived with Larry and Marie and Buck and Edna. With Steve's traveling schedule, we didn't see each other much, and when he came home for three or four days out of the month, I wanted to spend every minute with him.

The couple that lived in the duplex next to us had a little girl, and I agreed to watch her during the day while they were at work. They were supposed to pay me, but they never did. I didn't mind. Yolanda was two and a half years old, with silky black hair and the longest eyelashes I'd ever seen, and when she nestled in my lap with my arms curled protectively around her, something deep in my belly stirred with a yearning that felt as physical as hunger. Sometimes that craving would wake me up in the middle of the night, and I'd find myself squeezing the pillow with a ferocious longing so acute it made me ache. I couldn't talk myself out of it, couldn't fix it, and I couldn't escape it.

My friend Patty was pregnant. Steve and I had known Bob

and Patty back when we all worked at the dealership together in Missouri, and after we moved Bob decided he and Patty would move to Michigan too. Within two weeks Bob found a place for them to live in Holt, just a few miles away from us, and he went to work for a dealership in Lansing. It was nice having friends that weren't family living near us. Bob was twenty some years older than Patty, and she seemed to get pregnant as soon as he looked at her.

Just watching her belly grow larger month by month stirred my hormones to fever pitch, and made me long for a child of my own. She strutted around proud as a peacock, and took every opportunity to lean against doorframes to show off the ripening curve of her baby-to-be. I never told her how I felt—why rain on her parade?—but the sight of her pregnant belly triggered a nearly unbearable longing in me. My womb tugged at me all day, pulling at me with a misery I couldn't appease. I felt hollow, empty, and I wanted to be filled up.

I tried to keep busy with projects. Steve came up with an idea about how to make a ring from a silver quarter, and I spent hours and hours working on it. We used a Canadian quarter because I was worried about defacing U.S. currency—Steve didn't care about that, but I did—and besides, the Canadian quarter had a higher silver content, so it was easier to tap it into the shape of a ring. I held the quarter between my thumb and index finger of my left hand and tapped it with a spoon with my right hand. I tapped a little and turned it just a hair and tapped some more. My thumb and finger cramped from being in the same position for so long. I had to be careful and try to tap with the same pressure each time, because if I didn't, it was uneven. I tapped away at that quarter for months until the rim was flat and the width I wanted. When I finally finished it, Steve took it to work, drilled out the middle and polished it.

On each one of Steve's trips he brought back a surprise gift for me, and the night before my birthday we were snuggled up on the couch, basking in the luxury of a night to ourselves, when he reached into a brown paper bag next to the couch and pulled out a pair of ceramic figures of an old man and woman that he'd picked up at a truck stop.

When I turned the figurines over in my hands he smiled at me, kissed my cheek and said "This will be us thirty years from now."

Those little figurines sure looked married to me, and if they were supposed to be us thirty years from now, then Steve saw the future the same way I did. In my heart I was already married to him, and I wanted the outer reality to match this inner one. I wanted everything that went with marriage, and I needed to know Steve loved me enough and felt secure enough in our relationship to marry again.

Most of all, I needed to know he was over Dorothy.

I wanted to be Mrs. Milks.

On my birthday morning, sunlight danced through the shadows of the leaves on the tree outside our window, making wind-tossed patterns on the bedspread as I stared at the ceramic couple on my nightstand. My chest felt full of love and longing, and the light in the room seemed to enter me and radiate out of every pore.

I bent over Steve's sleeping face and tickled his ear. "I've been thinking."

He opened one sleepy eye and stared at me. "That's scary."

"Will you marry me, Stephen?"

He opened both eyes and stared at me for about ten seconds. "Are you *trying* to scare me?"

Unfazed by his reaction, I stretched back with my fingers laced together to cradle my head against the pillow. "I've waited long enough for you and Dorothy to settle the divorce. All that's left for her to do is pay off the lawyer so he can file it with the court. It's time to move on."

Steve propped himself up on one elbow to look down at my face. "When did this come up? You never said a word about it last night."

"I've always wanted to marry you. I thought about it every single time I tapped that ring with a spoon. Ever since the night Sue discovered us in bed and yanked the covers off us, I've been thinking about it. I never forgot what you told her: *If I'm going to marry anyone, it will be that girl in my bed.*"

He lifted a strand of hair away from my cheek, then smoothed the skin with his fingertips. "That's right. *If* I was going to marry anybody, you'd be the one I'd choose. You're my girl, Peep. You're my one and only. I come home to you every chance I get, turn over my paycheck to you so you can pay the bills and save us some money. I support you one hundred percent. Isn't that enough? Why do we need a piece of paper from the state of Michigan?"

I smiled serenely. "I'm going to marry you, Stephen."

He rolled his eyes toward the ceiling, gave me a brisk, businesslike kiss, then leapt out of bed and disappeared into the bathroom.

After I heard the toilet flush I followed him in there and sat on the edge of the tub while he washed his hands at the sink.

"October twenty-ninth," I told him. "Remember that date, because it's going to be your wedding day."

There was no special reason I picked that date, no sentimental value attached to it, but I knew it would give us time to get ready. "I'll set up an appointment so we can take our blood tests, and you and Dorothy can settle the divorce."

He raised his dripping hands from the sink and eyed me in the mirror. "You're serious."

I gazed at him calmly. "I am."

His eyes narrowed. "There's no way I'd ever set foot in a church to get married."

"We'll go to the courthouse. All we need is a judge and two witnesses. I'll ask Bob and Patty to come along and stand up for us."

Steve bent down over the sink, turned on both taps full blast and splashed water on his face. When he finally came up for air he grabbed a hand towel from the rack and spent a long time drying his face before he tossed it down on the counter.

I took a deep breath and kept on talking. "I want my last name to be the same as yours. What's wrong with that? I love you, and I know you love me. I want to be like that little old lady figurine you brought me last night. I want to grow old with you."

He groaned out loud. "The last marriage nearly killed me. I'm not about to go through all that again."

I smiled to soften the words, but there was steel in my voice.

"If you don't marry me, you're going to lose me."

I knew that if I didn't push him, we would never have a wedding. He just needed to figure out things between us wouldn't change once the ring was on my finger. That may have happened in his first marriage, and I could understand why he was worried about returning to the knock-down-drag-out fights that he and Dorothy went through after they married. But I also knew he was too comfortable with our lives the way they were.

I rose and stood next to him in front of the mirror and stared at our reflection. His blue eyes remained wary, while mine were filled with the shining light of my birthday morning conviction.

He faced me then, put his hands on my shoulders and gave me his big blue-eyed look, the one he used when he wanted me to give in to him, the one that always made me melt. "We've been getting along so good, babe. Why tinker with perfection?"

He's scared, I thought, and the realization filled me with tenderness. I made my voice low and gentle, as if I were comforting Stephanie or Stevie. "Our lives won't be any different than they are now. Don't you know that? But I need the commitment, Stephen. If you don't talk to Dorothy, I will."

He dropped his arms, turned and met my eyes in the mirror. "I don't like this," he muttered. His voice held the same note of resignation he used when I cornered him into taking out the garbage on a rainy night. "I don't like it at all."

I guess that's a yes, I thought. A pang of regret squeezed my heart at the memory of all the romantic proposals I'd seen in the movies, where the hero gets down on one knee to ask for the girl's hand in marriage before he whisks her off her feet and carries her away. But I knew Steve would never do that. It was up to me to make my dreams come true. If I wanted to get married, I'd have to orchestrate, conduct and play all the instruments to make this wedding happen.

I'd already made the ring. Now all I had to do was get Steve to show up on October 29 and put it on my finger.

Once I chose that date, I was adamant about it. I was getting married on October 29 and there was no changing this date and nothing would stand in the way. Years later Steve would tell friends the story and say, "October 29, she was getting married, come hell or high water."

In the end, I was the one who went to Dorothy to tell her Steve and I were going to marry. Up until then she'd always stalled because of the two hundred dollars she needed to pay her attorney to file the paperwork for the divorce, and she and Steve both seemed content to let it go.

After a whole year of scrimping and saving, I finally had the money for the lawyer to file the papers.

When I placed the check on the kitchen table and explained what the money was for, Dorothy sat down on her kitchen chair and sagged. Tears welled up in her eyes, and she blinked them away and swallowed hard. Her face suddenly looked about ten years older.

"It's hard for me, you know? We've been married since I was sixteen. Steve was my first love. Finalizing the divorce … it just feels like we failed." She waved a hand in front of her face to fan away the tears. "I know it's stupid."

I reached forward in my chair and hugged her tightly. "I'm sorry, Dorothy." I liked her so much. She'd been a good friend to me, and I hated to cause her pain. I loved her kids as if they were my own, and we'd given each other a lot of love and moral support over the past two years. "But you can understand why I'd want to be his wife, can't you?"

She let out a humorless laugh. "Steve always said if he ever married again, it would be you. Don't mind me, Penny. I just need to feel it for a while."

"So you'll do it?" I asked. "You'll pay the lawyer and tell him to file the papers?"

She gave me an amused look. "You got it bad, don't you? Those old wedding bell blues?"

I shrugged. "I've waited long enough. I want to be his wife. It's time for me to be Mrs. Milks."

She shook a cigarette out of her pack, lit a match and blew smoke at the ceiling. "You'll never get him to go for a church wedding."

Dorothy didn't have to rub it in. I knew there would be no church wedding for me, no white dress, no cake, no bridesmaids or rice thrown at us as we made our honeymoon getaway. There would be no honeymoon, period. I would have to take whatever I could get.

I want the marriage, I thought. *Nothing else matters.*

In late October I dragged Steve to a family practice in Holt for our blood tests for the license. Since we were both healthy, we hadn't been there before and didn't know any of the doctors, so one was assigned to give us a general exam and draw our blood.

We were told it would take three days for the results.

Three days later I was just mixing up a batch of brownies for the kids when the phone rang. I licked the spatula while the nurse from the doctor's office identified herself and asked if she could speak to Steve.

"He's at work," I told her. "Can I help? I'm his fiancée."

"We'd like to talk to him about his test results. Could you ask him to call us when he gets home?"

I dropped the spatula in the sink and set the pot on the counter. "Is he sick? Is there something wrong?"

"Just have him call us." She gave me the number, thanked me and hung up.

I held the phone and stared into the mouthpiece as if the dial tone might tell me something more if I listened hard enough, then slowly placed the receiver back on the cradle.

When Steve came home, I didn't even wait for him to kiss me hello. I gave him the doctor's number and told him to call.

He picked up the receiver and dialed, then leaned against the kitchen counter and waited for the receptionist to transfer him to the nurse. He winked at me, took his wallet out of his back pocket and tossed it on the kitchen counter with the loose change and car keys from his front pockets.

Too nervous to stand still, I pulled some hamburger out of the refrigerator, lit the burner on the stove and slid a frying pan over it while I listened to his side of the conversation.

After he identified himself to the nurse he listened to her for a while before he said "Positive! What's that mean?"

A long silence ensued.

"But I don't have any symptoms," he said. "Are you sure?"

Another long pause.

"Both of us? Why?"

I poured some Mazola in the pan and ripped the cellophane off the meat.

"Okay, when?"

He scribbled something on the note pad next to the phone. "Yeah. Okay. Thanks."

He hung up the phone and stared at the piece of paper as if it were a dog that had bit him.

"What is it?" I asked.

He shook his head. "My blood test came back positive for the fucking clap. Can you fucking believe this?"

I stared at him. "What does that mean?"

"It means venereal disease, that's what it means. I tested positive for gonorrhea, and now they want both of us to come in tomorrow."

Suddenly I couldn't breathe. It felt like a strand of wire had wrapped around my heart and cinched it tight. "How did you get venereal disease?"

He glowered at the phone before he sat down heavily on the stool by the counter. "They must be wrong. I don't have any symptoms, and I sure as hell haven't done anything to get it since we met."

I stared at him, measuring his expression. He looked irritated more than anything, without a speck of guilt or shame in his face. If he were lying to me he'd probably make a joke out of it and try to snuggle up to me, but he just looked pissed off.

I desperately wanted to believe him. But then there were all those long nights I'd spent here in the duplex while he was out drinking with dealers and sales people on the road, sleeping in a strange bed every night. *Whose bed?* Temptation was everywhere, and I knew he loved sex. *What happens when he's drunk and horny and a thousand miles away from home?*

When we went for our appointment the next morning, the doctor explained the disease and the symptoms. Steve was right about one thing, he did not have the symptoms: no burning sensation when urinating, no discharge, no pain or swelling in his testicles.

"Why didn't I get it?" I asked the doctor. "My test came back negative, and we've had an active sex life for two years."

"*Very* active," Steve said.

The doctor spread his hands open in a gesture of apology. "Who knows? It happens this way sometimes."

"I don't see how I could have this thing," Steve told the doctor. "Your lab must have made a mistake."

"It's possible. You could repeat the test, if you want. Or you could both get a shot of penicillin right now and be done with it."

Steve shook his head in disgust and looked at me. "You're the one who would wonder if I really had it, Peep. You want to just get the shot?"

I sat there and stared at Steve for several long seconds. If we were going to get married on October 29, there wasn't enough time for another test. This test may have given him a false positive, but if he did have a venereal disease then we should both have the injection.

Damn it, I thought. *I am getting married, clap or no clap.*

I took a shaky breath and nodded. "Give us the shot. Let's

get it over with."

When we left the doctor's office, my behind felt like it had been stung by a wasp. Steve was quiet as we drove away in the car. I counted the telephone poles going by, too upset to talk. Neither of us said a word until Steve pulled into our driveway and parked the car in front of the duplex.

"If you had sex with someone else, you need to make a call," I told him.

"Point taken," Steve said. "Now let's drop it, okay?"

Thank goodness marriage counseling wasn't required back then. I don't think Steve would have tolerated it.

On the morning of October 29, Steve paced the rooms, fiddled with the doors and windows and opened and closed all the drawers in the kitchen, too nervous and keyed up to sit still. He tried to cover it by spitting out one-liners about how he was walking toward the "wedding noose," how I was sentencing him to "marriage without parole," and the judge was about to pronounce him "ninety-nine to life."

By now I knew he used sarcasm and jokes to cover his nerves, but each little comment felt like a thorn that prickled and burned its way under my skin.

This is my wedding day, I thought. *Why can't he see that I might be nervous too?* I wished that he had thought to give me flowers, at least. I'd let go of all the other traditions. My pink and white patterned dress wasn't white, or even new. There was nothing borrowed, nothing blue, and I didn't even think about him seeing the bride before the wedding. He wasn't the least bit interested in what I looked like, and I was so focused on trying to calm him that I just wanted the whole thing to be over and done with.

He spent a long time sprucing himself up in the mirror before he pulled on a cream colored suit with brown top stitching that outlined his pockets, collar and lapels. It took him three tries to knot his dark brown silk tie. When the tie was finally straight he lifted its tail over his head to imitate being strangled while he bugged his eyes at me in the bathroom mirror.

It wasn't vanity that had him glued to the mirror—he was just downright scared.

I wasn't nervous about marrying him, but I was terrified of going to the courthouse and talking to a judge. And just watching Steve was making me nervous. My hands shook as I wriggled my toe into the leg of my brand new pantyhose and pulled the nylon up over my thigh. Even though it was forty degrees outside, perspiration bloomed on my face as I pulled on my brassiere and slip, and I had to towel off my underarms before I was ready to step into my dress. By then my palms were slippery with sweat.

At long last we left the duplex to drive to the courthouse. The whole way there I watched Steve out of the corner of my eye, halfway expecting him to make a U-turn and take us both back home. By the time he pulled into a parking space, though, it seemed like he'd calmed down a little. He pulled the keys out of the ignition, sat back in his seat and gave me a smile, the first real smile he'd given me all day. "You ready to get this thing done?"

My pulse quickened, and I nodded.

Bob and Patty were already waiting at the door to the courthouse, grinning so hard it made me even more jumpy than I already was. Bob wore a western suit complete with a string tie and cowboy hat. Patty was nine months pregnant, and her belly was enormous, a fifty pound curve she held with both hands as she waddled through the door.

Steve held the door open for me and offered his arm in a gallant flourish. I slipped my hand through the crook of his elbow and he escorted me down the oak-lined corridor to the clerk's office. For the first time that day I began to feel like a real bride, walking carefully down the hallway to the wedding march playing in my mind.

The waiting room was full of people, young couples, old people and small children milling around, and it took a while for us to make our way to the window where we checked in with a secretary wearing bifocals and a big beehive hairdo.

Steve greeted her in his best salesman's voice. "Good morning! How are you doing? I'm Steve Milks, and this is my fiancée Penny. We're here to get married."

"Yahoo!" Bob whooped, and Patty giggled and dug her elbow into his side.

The secretary stared at us over her bifocals and said "Do you have an appointment?"

"No," I said. "Do we need one?"

"I'm sorry," she said. "We're really booked. The judge is in court right now, and his allotted times for meetings are filled."

"You mean …he won't be able to marry us?"

She lifted her hands and gave us a helpless shrug of apology. "Not today, honey."

I froze. *Not today?* I'd gone through all this *for nothing?*

I staggered a little and held the counter to steady myself, while disappointment crashed over me like a tidal wave. It never dawned on me that the judge wouldn't have time to marry us.

They never mentioned making an appointment when we applied for the marriage license, and I just assumed it was first come, first serve.

My heart thudded dully in my ears, and before I could gather myself together, my eyes stung with tears. I'd been so sure this would be the day I would finally become Mrs. Milks. This was the day I knew in my heart was supposed to be my wedding day. How could I be so wrong?

Tears streamed down my cheeks and I didn't even lift a hand to wipe them away. I turned to Steve, half blind and heartbroken.

Steve looked at me with infinite sadness, his eyes full of compassion. He knew what this wedding meant to me. He held my gaze and his eyes seemed to take on a darker color as his love for me shone through the sadness. Even in the middle of my own misery, I knew I'd never seen him look at me that way before.

He lifted a hand and gently wiped away my tears with his thumb.

"Patty," he said, without taking his gaze away from mine. "Call the pastor at your church. See if your minister can marry us today."

Patty gave him a nod, fished a dime out of her purse and waddled down the corridor to the pay phone.

"You'd marry me in church?" I asked in a shaky voice.

He kissed my forehead. "It's time you made an honest man of me, Peep. Today's going to be our wedding day." He laughed and kissed me on the lips. "Come on, let's see what Patty can do for us."

"Mr. Milks?"

We turned to see the face with the bifocals and the beehive hairdo back at the window, beaming at us.

"Yes?" Steve said.

"I just spoke to the judge and explained your situation. The court is in recess, and he said he'd come over and marry you right now. Are you ready?"

I clutched Steve's hand and we exchanged a look. In my mind I could hear Wagner's Bridal March, the organ notes ascending in a bright command to walk together to the moment when our lives would be legally, spiritually and physically linked together forever and ever. My take-charge husband-to-be smiled down at me, his face alight with love and happiness.

"You want to get this thing done?" I asked him.

"I do," he said.

❧ *Chapter Seven* ❧

In 1978 Champion offered Steve a sales manager position in Canastota, New York. At long last, his road trips were over! I'd turned twenty-one the year before—legal drinking age at last—while Steve was thirty-eight and just beginning to worry about turning forty. We'd been married for almost two years, and I was ecstatic at the thought of him coming home to me every night instead of knowing he was sitting in a bar a thousand miles away and going to sleep without me in a motel bed.

Champion was opening a new plant in Canastota to fill the demand for the TransVan, their newest vehicle. At the time it was one of the hottest vehicles in the RV industry, an "upsized van" that provided a smaller, sleeker, sexier version of the larger Class A motor homes that had been the mainstay of the Champion line-up.

In August 1978, Steve found a townhouse for us to rent and we moved from Michigan to Canastota, New York. Our townhouse sat back off the highway in a picturesque country setting, up on the crown of a hill that sloped down steeply in the back. The interior featured three levels, with a sliding glass door off the dining room that offered a view of the enormous old maple and oak trees that surrounded the property. A month after we moved in, the autumn color in those changing leaves lit up the hills in flaming gold and red, and I woke up every morning to a view that was pretty as a postcard.

The kids were none too thrilled about our move—no more weekly trips to the candy store, no more outings with Steve when he was home from a road trip, and no more playtime with me on the weekends he was gone—but when they came to visit us in Canastota for Christmas we all had a blast. They loved sledding down the big hill in back of the apartment. I liked it too, although it was a long hard walk back up to the top, and Steve preferred to watch from the toasty warmth of the townhouse. We had a wonderful vacation, and Stephanie and Stevie were sad to go home.

I liked moving, starting all over, having a new place to decorate and new places to explore. The whole country seemed to be in a good mood. A gallon of gas cost sixty-two cents, and the average family income was about seventeen thousand dollars a year. According to the social security worksheets I've kept on file ever since we married, Steve made $17,700 that year, so we were feeling prosperous at last.

Our year in Canastota went by quickly, but oh, what fun we had! Looking back, that year was probably the first time I realized a person could be a responsible citizen during the day, and go out and have a rip-roaring good time partying at night.

Right across the highway from our townhouse was a bar/restaurant named Club 44, and Steve had a standing order with me: "If I'm not home by six, come to the bar."

We spent almost every night at Club 44, and eventually we became good friends with the owners, Marsh and Gini. Marsh was short and stocky, a little gruff in a nice, soft spoken sort of way. Never loud, but if he wanted someone to listen, they did. Anyone could see that Marsh and Gini were totally in love with each other, and I always had the impression that he would do anything for her. Gini was petite, with short dark curly hair, a sweet woman and a hard worker. While Marsh ran the bar, Gini was always in motion, greeting people, waitressing or helping out in the kitchen.

In the early spring of 1979, on a chilly night in mid-April, Steve called to tell me to meet him at the bar. As usual, I was eager to see him and spent a long time getting ready for our evening at the club. During the day I'd cleaned the house, done the laundry, ironed all his dress shirts, and spent the afternoon baking cupcakes. When I wasn't doing household chores I loved to bake and do crafts, but it was lonely work. I was ready for a night of drinking, conversation and play.

I showered, applied fresh lipstick, blush, eyeliner and mascara, changed into a fresh pair of jeans and a clean blouse and put on the first piece of jewelry Steve had ever given me, a necklace with a pendant shaped like a small gold key with a tiny diamond on it. When he'd given me the box on Christmas morning he smiled and said "It's the key to my heart." I wore it every day.

After I brushed my hair, checked myself in the mirror one more time and slipped into my overcoat, I headed outside. Fat snowflakes were just beginning to fall, and I shivered as I hurried to my Buick Electra in the driveway.

This car was my prized possession, the first car we'd owned together, and I was proud of myself for picking it out and handling the whole deal while Steve was on one of his last road trips for the company. It wasn't brand new when I bought it, but the mileage was low and it was in perfect shape, a real creampuff and a steal at $7500. Dark mahogany brown, powered by a 455 engine with a respectable 315 horsepower, the Electra drove like a Cadillac, with cushy seats and a body as big and long as a land yacht.

I'd just sent in the final payment for the Electra the month before, and the title had arrived by certified mail that very afternoon. As I pulled out of the driveway and nosed the Electra across the highway to Club 44, I was sure I was driving the classiest car on the road and all the other drivers envied me. Steve usually drove a TransVan that Champion provided for him, so the Electra was my baby.

By now Club 44 felt like our home away from home, and I felt a tingle of anticipation as soon as I walked in the door and inhaled the familiar smells of steak and onion rings sizzling in the kitchen, with the yeasty aroma of beer wafting from the bar. Rod Stewart's voice came blasting through the speakers, singing "Tonight's the Night," and I shimmied over and slid a few quarters into the jukebox to line up Kenny Rogers' "Lucille," Fleetwood Mac's "Go Your Own Way," and Ronnie Milsap's "It Was Almost Like A Song"—all the songs we loved and played in our apartment.

Since it was Friday night, the Club was already beginning to fill up, and I surveyed the crowd for faces I knew. Seven or eight people sat at the cocktail tables, while another half dozen congregated at the bar where Marsh stood in his shirtsleeves and apron, mixing drinks. The dark paneled walls enclosed us in a small space that made it easy to rub elbows and get to know your neighbor, and I paused to say hello to the people I'd met over the long winter. Busboys, waiters and waitresses circulated through the bar and the restaurant, clearing away glasses and fetching drinks and food for the customers. A pleasant buzz of laughter and the click of balls on the pool table floated over the room, and I could feel the glow of the weekend ahead in the atmosphere. The air itself seemed to shine with expectation.

When Gini caught sight of me she opened her arms to give me a quick hug even though she was in the middle of showing customers to their table in the restaurant. "You look fresh as a daisy!" she said, and looked me up and down. "What's your secret?"

"Clean living, I guess," I said. "Washing windows, vacuuming, scrubbing the kitchen floor and all that laundry—it's as good as a workout with Jack LaLanne."

She laughed and moved off with her customers while I made my way to my preferred spot at the bar, in the back corner against the wall, where I had a view out the picture window for Steve's TransVan when it pulled into the parking lot.

Marsh slapped a coaster down on the bar and leaned toward me. "What'll it be, Penny?" His eyes twinkled behind his oversized tortoiseshell spectacles.

"Vodka and grapefruit juice, please. Any sign of Steve yet?"

"Not yet. You're all mine until he gets here, so buckle your seat belt." Within half a minute he had the drink assembled, and placed the frosty glass of juice and vodka in front of me.

Marsh hummed along to Kenny Rogers as he cleared away a few beer bottles, dumped them in the bin below the bar and wiped the counter with a rag to clean up the rings of moisture they'd left behind.

"You're in a cheerful mood," I said, and took a sip of my drink. "What's up?"

Marsh lifted his chin toward the pool table. "You see those kids? They've had just enough Jack Daniels to think they're good."

"Ah." I took another sip and studied the newcomers. Dressed in work boots, blue jeans and plaid flannel shirts, they looked like they were about my age, no more than twenty-two or twenty-three years old. One freckled redhead, one blonde. Good looking boys from upstate New York, with ruddy sunburned faces—probably field workers in the local onion fields. Something in the way they flashed covert glances at me and talked a little louder than necessary made me think they might be screwing up their courage to approach me.

I held the glass with my left hand and made no effort to hide my wedding band. Wedding band or no wedding band, I knew these boys would never approach me, because no one ever tried to pick me up while I waited for Steve at the bar. It irritated me sometimes how women would flirt with Steve like crazy, but men would just ignore me. I asked Steve once why no men ever tried to pick me up, and he said "It's just the way you are, Peeps. You give off this 'Don't Touch Me' vibe, and men can feel it. If you ever smiled at them or gave them some friendly eye contact they'd be all over you."

The kids at the pool table looked like they'd just collected their paychecks and headed to the bar with a fistful of cash, ready for a big night on the town.

I turned back to Marsh. "You think they're looking for some action?"

"Steve could wipe the floor with them," he said. "Like taking candy from a baby."

Marsh knew Steve had more finesse on the pool table than any of his other customers, and he often staked him to play matches for anything up to a hundred dollars per game. That was a lot of money back in those days, but Steve was an incredible player.

"Speak of the devil," Marsh said softly.

Steve stood framed in the doorway and grinned at us while snowflakes whirled around him, and a burst of cold air blew into the room.

My chest swelled with happiness at the sight of him as the first wave of tipsiness from the vodka poured through me. He always looked so good to me. It filled me up just to see his face, and this warm heat rose up in me every time he walked in the door. It was like Christmas, my birthday and the fourth of July all rolled up in one to know that this gorgeous man was my husband. To me he was always the most handsome, charismatic man in the place.

Before Steve crossed the room to take his seat next to me at the bar he paused at the pool table and put two quarters on the rail to challenge the kid who was winning. They exchanged a few words and then Steve made his way toward me, his eyebrows lifted in greeting.

He gave me a quick kiss hello before he loosened his tie, took off his jacket and slid onto the bar stool next to me. "What's the haps, Peep? You got an early start on me?"

I lifted my drink in response, then leaned over to inhale the scent of his skin and the lingering trace of cologne that remained after a day working the sales desk. He smelled wonderful to me, and he was always impeccably dressed. In the past year he'd grown a beard, and I thought it made him look distinguished, even though he fretted over the gray hairs that were just beginning to appear in it. All winter long he'd brooded obsessively about turning forty. Once after a long night of drinking he got so pissed off at the wrinkles he saw in the mirror that he punched his fist through the bathroom door. He went out the next day and bought wrinkle cream, then had a perm put in his hair at my hair salon. I still laugh at the thought of him in a beauty shop with perm rods in his hair. This all happened in January, so his hair had grown out, and that night he just had a cute little wave on the ends.

"The usual?" Marsh asked Steve, his hand poised over the bottle of Absolut.

"What the hell, it's Friday night, make it scotch," Steve said.

Whenever he drank scotch I always held my breath, because scotch seemed to make him behave even more recklessly than usual. For Steve, that was saying something. I could tell from the gleam in his eye that we were in for an eventful night.

Marsh and Steve and I chatted until the pool game ended, and then Steve hoisted himself off his bar stool to pick up a cue stick. After I watched him play a few sloppy games of eight ball to lull the farm boys into a false sense of security, I wandered over to the bowling machine to sharpen my skills.

The bowling machine was a long table, two and a half feet wide and nine or ten feet long, with a bed of polished pine, just like a bowling lane. When I put two quarters in the machine the pins would drop down, and I'd pick up my flat steel "ball," which was shaped like a hockey puck, and slide the puck down the table, aiming at the pins. There was no prize, other than the satisfaction of beating the person you were playing or the satisfaction of a strike or a perfect game. I loved this bar game, and spent hours absorbed in it.

When I'd spent my last quarter I looked back toward the pool table and saw Steve pick up his cue stick with a tight, focused mask of determination on his face. *Now the game really begins,* I thought. It seemed as though all the sounds and sights and smells of the bar fell away from him, until he was alone in a universe of geometry and angles and planes that I couldn't begin to understand. It was a thrill to watch him, but it was also a little eerie. His power of concentration seemed so strong that I could have sworn he was *thinking* the ball into its pocket through sheer willpower. Bank shots, combinations, caroms, jump shots and curve balls—he could do them all, and give the cue ball exactly the right English to make it roll into the position he needed for the next shot. In less than a minute he ran the table.

The farm kids looked thunderstruck, as if they'd been hit by a force of nature that left them shaken and more than a little scared. Steve shook hands with both of them before they finally turned tail and ran off.

Steve waved a fistful of bills at Marsh, and I went over to join them at the bar and have a drink to celebrate. We huddled over the bar while Marsh counted out the bills with a big beaming smile on his face, and I nuzzled Steve's cheek.

"How much did you win?" I whispered.

He shrugged. "Couple hundred, more or less. Enough for a little poker stake."

"Three hundred and seventy-five dollars!" Marsh cackled. "A great night, and it's just getting started." He dealt out a stack of bills to Steve, who pocketed them quietly with a secret look of satisfaction.

As he did almost every evening around closing time, Marsh pulled a deck of cards from the cash register, and we all bellied up to the bar to play a poker game called Acey Deucey. Even though I'd never been good at cards, I was addicted to the game and the late-night excitement it could spark.

Here's how the game worked: Marsh dealt one card face-up to each player including himself. Then he dealt a second card face-up to the player to the left. Before any more cards were dealt, that player would bet whether or not his next card off the top of the deck would be a number that fell between the first two cards. After the bet was made, Marsh gave the player another card, face-up. If the player's first two cards were a two and a ten, and the next card was an eight, that player would collect the amount that he bet from the pot. If the next card was a jack, that player would have to pay the amount he bet into the pot. If the next card was a two or a ten, the player "hit the post" and had to pay double the amount that he'd bet into the pot.

After a night of hard drinking, the pots bloomed quickly into a sizable chunk of money. It was pretty exciting. Half the time I didn't know what I was doing, but Steve did, and he coached me. With alcohol involved, you just never knew what was going to happen. Of course, Steve liked gambling and pretty soon I discovered that I liked it too, even though it made me so nervous I could hardly stand to look at my cards.

On this night, though, the betting got completely out of hand. One by one the other players quit until only Marsh, Steve and I and a regular named Gus were left with a pot that held more money than we'd ever seen on the line. After one spectacular round of bets where we all hit the post, the pot held a couple thousand dollars.

By then I had put away about three or four vodkas with grapefruit juice, way past the limit I allowed myself when I planned to drive home. Tonight I'd stagger back to the townhouse on foot, and make Steve walk with me. My Electra could sit in the parking lot until tomorrow.

When Gus hit the post again he took off his wristwatch—a Rolex, with a gold and platinum wristband—and threw it on the pile. There was a suppressed murmur in the knot of people around us, and a few more waiters and busboys drifted into the bar to see what was going on.

When it was my turn to bet I pushed my cards back toward Marsh, waved them away and said "Fuck this, I'm out."

Steve winked at Marsh and said "I can always tell when she's had too much to drink—she waves her hands higher in the air and she says 'fuck.' "

"It's up to you," Gus said to Steve. "You in or out?"

"You want to front me some cash, Marsh?" Steve asked.

"Not a chance," Marsh laughed. "You already bet all the money you won at the pool table. This is getting way too rich for my blood."

Steve took a thoughtful sip of his scotch and water, then placed the glass back down on the bar. Moving slowly, as if he had all the time in the world, he shook a cigarette out of his pack, stuck it between his lips, took a book of matches from the bar, scratched a match and touched the flame to the tip of the cigarette until it glowed red.

"You have the keys to the Electra?" he asked me.

Where are you going? I wondered. "Sure."

He exhaled a plume of smoke and held his hand out, and I automatically groped in my purse for the car keys and placed them in his waiting palm.

Without hesitating, Steve slapped the keys on top of the pot, took another belt of scotch and maintained his deadpan expression, but his eyes shone with a devilish fuck-it-all gleam. He had a two and a seven of clubs showing, and if the next card wasn't a three, four, five or six, my beloved Buick Electra would be lost. No one in their right mind would ever make that bet.

"Jesus Mary and Joseph!" Marsh exclaimed. "Now we got ourselves a game."

The handful of customers who were still seated in the bar all stood up and walked over to watch, while Gini and a few waitresses materialized to witness the fate of the high stakes pot. Up until that moment I had no idea so many people were still in the club, but every one of them had sensed the rising tension at the bar and come out to see the floor show.

The haze of vodka made everything seem removed, as if I were watching a movie unfold in slow motion, but even through the cocoon of alcohol I felt weak at the thought of giving up my car. It seemed impossible. If Steve lost, would Gus really drive off in my beautiful Electra?

I placed my hand on top of the pot to stall the game. My car keys felt hard and reassuringly solid under my hand, and I hated to let them go.

I whispered in Steve's ear. "What if we lose?"

Steve took another drag of his cigarette, kept his eyes on the cards and never even glanced up at me. "It's like money in the bank, Peeps. Trust me. I got my Super Folium Adjustment Factor all lined up on this baby."

The Super Folium Adjustment Factor was a phrase Steve had made up to calm nervous buyers, but it didn't cut any ice with me.

When I didn't remove my hand, he looked up at me at last. "Come on, P. It's not in the river but I got it dragged to the bank. You see the size of that pot? Let him deal the damn card and we'll be fartin' through velvet."

I didn't budge, and I enunciated every word with care. "What. If. You. Lose?"

He held my gaze, cool as Cool Hand Luke, completely unperturbed by the crowd that surrounded him. "We'll be looking for you a new ride tomorrow." He tapped the ash from his cigarette into the tin ashtray at his elbow, then offered me the lit cigarette.

Marsh and Gini exchanged a look, eyebrows raised.

"Go on," Gus said, licking his lips to smother a smile. I knew he was salivating at the thought of driving off in my Electra. "Deal the damn cards and put us out of our misery."

Everyone was waiting for me to move my hand away from the pot, and I could feel them watching, whispering, pressing closer around me. *There was a protocol about this kind of thing, wasn't there?* Once a bet was made, you couldn't take it back. Not even if your husband was about seven sheets to the wind and had just bet your car on a poker game.

From the minute I met Steve, it felt like he was tugging me into deep water, way over my head, out of my comfort zone, toward risk and opportunity and the possibility of disaster. It always left me with this anxious roiling in my gut as I desperately searched for a safe place in the wake of his choices. From the beginning, he'd been a gambler, a risk taker, and I hated this overwhelmingly familiar feeling of helplessness as he dragged me into the deep end. For years I'd tried to manage him, I tried to control him, I'd kick him under the table until his shins were black and blue when he drank too much and pissed off the wrong people, but ultimately he would do whatever he wanted anyway and there wasn't a damn thing I could do about it. He didn't care that I was the one who would have to live with the consequences if he lost this bet. His recklessness was part of what made him Steve.

All these thoughts ran through my head in the time it took to blink. I stared at him, torn by the impulse to give in to him and the urge to stay safe.

Slowly, reluctantly, I lifted my hand from the pot, plucked the cigarette from his fingers and took a long shaky inhale. *Even if we don't win, it'll make a hell of a story,* I thought.

Marsh flipped the top card in the deck over. It was the five of diamonds.

The room erupted in cheers and applause. "Thank you baby Jesus!" I squealed, and hopped off my bar stool to hug Steve.

"Just like downtown," Steve said, and scraped the pot with the watch and the car keys toward himself with both hands.

Even Gus had to laugh at the grand finale to the biggest pot ever bet at Club 44, and he patted me on the back and shook Steve's hand. "*Hell* of a game, Steve. You must have the luck of the angels."

Steve stood up from his stool, took the watch from the pile of money and slid it into Gus's shirt pocket. Then he grinned at me, gave me a kiss and whispered in my ear, "You're the only angel I need."

After that the pot seemed to disappear before my eyes as Steve passed out twenty dollar bills across the bar to Gini and Marsh and all the waitresses and busboys and onlookers who had come out to watch the fun. Steve loved tipping, and he loved to watch the expression on the face of the person he was tipping. When he was still on the road for Champion, traveling from state to state and reporting his per diem expenses, the company fined him for over-tipping. He always claimed he was "making up for all the cheap sons-of-bitches who didn't leave anything."

"That's just for showing up," he said to everyone as he poked twenty dollar bills into their shirt pockets, and they all laughed as they clapped him on the back, shook his hand, kissed his cheek and milled around us.

"Sprinkle the infield," Steve roared above the commotion. "Marsh, give us one for the ditch."

❧ *Chapter Eight* ❧

On a crisp autumn afternoon in 1983 I cut up a nice three pound fryer for our dinner. Steve and I had been married for seven years by now, and I knew it was true what they said about the way to a man's heart. The way to my man's heart was fried chicken and mashed potatoes with cream style corn poured over the potatoes, served with biscuits, butter and homemade strawberry jam. For dessert, a homemade apple pie with vanilla ice cream. Steve and I called this the "All-American Dinner."

The All-American Dinner had always been my good luck charm, and it had the power to put Steve in his happiest, most expansive and generous mood. Tonight I would make the best meal on earth for my man, and I prayed that it would be just like old times. We'd sit at the table and laugh and every forkful would make him groan because everything tasted so good.

Last night it was close to midnight before Steve sauntered in. He flung open the front door and let it slam shut, abruptly waking me out of my doze in front of Johnny Carson.

"Hey Peep, how goes the war?" His words were slurred, his eyes puffy.

"You're late."

" Don't watch the clock," he said with a half smile. "Watch the calendar."

He used this line sometimes when he left the house. I didn't think it was funny then and it sure wasn't funny now, but I knew better than to argue with him if he'd been drinking. He wouldn't remember a thing about this conversation in the morning, and I'd just be wasting my breath if I yelled at him.

This was the worst time in our marriage. Although we'd come through bad times before, I was seriously scared about our future together, and I wasn't sure I could fix it just by keeping my head down and giving him enough room to snap out of it. In the past I'd always had faith that things would improve. But now? I just didn't know.

Since 1979 we'd moved twice. Toward the end of June 1979 the price of gas nearly doubled from sixty cents to a dollar a gallon, and there were some regional gas shortages, which hit the RV industry hard. Steve had to fire dozens of people at the plant in Canastota, New York, and within a month the plant closed.

Champion transferred him back to Michigan, and we were both glad he still had a job with the same salary, in spite of the shakeup in the company. We lived in Lansing while Steve worked in Flint, an hour's drive away, where he ran the Champion Showcase retail lot on Dort Highway, and another in Detroit.

For a while, life continued to be as sweet as it had been in Canastota. We picked up Steph and Stevie regularly, and they loved having us back in Michigan. Our troubles began with Steve's hour-long drive to work, and his habit of going out to party with his sales staff in the evenings. His sales people at the Flint Showcase lot were a fun-loving group, and he knew all the local police and did a lot of drinking with them. One drink would have been fine. But that one drink turned into three or four, and then he'd climb behind the wheel of the TransVan and drive fifty miles home.

It was a harrowing experience to wait for him to come home every night. I spent a lot of time imagining the worst: the TransVan upended in a ditch, Steve carried away from the flaming wreck on a gurney, or led away from the scene in handcuffs by the police.

We both knew it was time to move closer to his work in Flint, so in 1980 we rented a tri-level house on Bridgeman Trail in Swartz Creek, a small town outside of Flint, just a few minutes away from the Champion showcase lot. We had three-quarters of an acre, with a nice big back yard that we loved and separate bedrooms for both of the kids when they came to visit.

Although we lived closer to his work, there were permanent knots in my shoulders from the tension I felt whenever he stayed out late to hit the bars with his sales crew. I couldn't count the number of times I begged him to call me for a ride, or at least find a motel where he could sober up before he drove home.

One night when I was getting ready for bed the phone rang and a woman told me my husband had wrecked his car. She said he had showed up at her door and wanted me to come and pick him up. After she gave me directions to her house on Hill Road, I grabbed Stephanie and we jumped in the Electra.

As soon as we crested the incline of Hill Road we saw the flashing lights of several police cars clustered around the TransVan, which had plowed into a guardrail. I was horrified by the sight of the crushed front end, out of my mind with worry. My stomach dropped out of my body, and my hands felt like ice.

Is he hurt? Where was he? Had they hauled him off to the

hospital, or thrown him in jail?

When I pulled over to talk to the police, a familiar figure loomed out of the strobe-lit darkness and walked up to our car. *Thank God!* I thought, and let out the breath I'd been holding ever since we saw the TransVan buried in the guardrail.

Lightheaded with relief, I jumped out and opened my arms to hug him. He reeked of alcohol.

He unhooked my arms from his neck and lightly pushed me away. "Did you bring me any coffee?"

"No, I didn't bring any coffee. I thought you might be hurt, or in jail. I just grabbed your daughter and ran."

"Jeeze! You drove right past me," he complained. "I had to walk a quarter mile."

Stung by his greeting, I backed away. *You should be hugging me with gratitude,* I thought. "You're okay? You're not under arrest?"

"Nah," he said breezily. "They said they'd let me go, as long as someone else drove me home. Let's blow this popsicle stand."

As far as I could tell, Steve didn't learn a thing from this episode. He went right on partying hard with his sales staff until May 1983, when an unexpected disaster brought the good times to a halt.

One morning Steve went off to work, and in the middle of the afternoon he came home. I saw his car roll up the drive to the attached garage, and a few minutes later I heard the door in the kitchen open and close. I called down to him from upstairs, where I'd been folding laundry. "How come you're home so early, baby? You want to fool around?"

When he came up the stairs and entered our bedroom he looked at me with a scowl, his blue eyes shooting sparks, his body tense as a wire. "They fired me."

The air felt heavy with the weight of his words, and I was so shocked I couldn't move. *Fired?* How could they fire their best salesman, their top manager, their number one fan? He'd been with Champion for eight years, played a major role in the launch of the TransVan, and everyone who worked with him knew there was no one who worked harder.

"You've got to be kidding me!" I said. "Why would they fire you?" I knew he never played the game of kissing up to his new boss at the corporate office. Steve said what he thought, and I'm sure that didn't go over well, but still! *Fired?*

"I'm going to bed," he said.

He stayed in bed for three days. For three days I catered to him, brought him meals and snacks, and he watched TV from morning to night. For hours every day I talked to him and tried everything to shake him out of his depression. Nothing worked.

On the morning of the fourth day I stood in the doorway of our bedroom and stared at the man who was curled up and snoring in bed at ten a.m. while the TV blared from the dresser. A dribble of saliva had coated one side of his mouth and made a wet spot on the pillow. His hair was plastered to one side of his head, and the room smelled like sweat, cigarette smoke and feet. I couldn't handle seeing him like this, and it was pretty clear it wasn't doing him any good to be pampered.

I crossed the room in two long strides and snapped the TV off.

"Hey," he muttered from the bed, his eyes still closed. "I was watching that."

I put my fists on my hips and spoke as loud as I dared. "Stephen A. Milks, you need to get over it. Lying around feeling sorry for yourself won't help. You need to get up and do something!"

He glared at me. "I'm not looking for another job."

"Fine," I told him. "But we'll need to eat when the money from your severance pay runs out. You're going to get the roto-tiller out of the garage and till up the back yard for me, because I'm going to plant a vegetable garden. Come on. The exercise will do you good."

He flung the covers back, sat on the edge of the bed and ran his fingers through his hair.

I plucked a freshly laundered T-shirt from the stack I'd just folded and threw it at his head. "Now, buddy."

He yawned and scratched his beard. I held my breath, afraid he might topple back into bed any second.

"Coffee first," he said. And then he stood up.

The truth was I loved having him at home that summer. Although he never really got over being fired, he cheered up after a few days. He built shelves for the living room, made us a dining room table and spent plenty of time working on his tan, as if he were on an extended vacation. We both knew that when he was ready to go back to work, he'd find a job. He was a great salesman, and the fact that he'd been fired hadn't made a dent in his charisma. Steve was still the same quick-witted, gorgeous man I fell in love with nine years earlier.

In the meantime he tilled the garden, and we grew everything that summer: green beans, peas, zucchini, squash, tomatoes, potatoes, onions, corn, green peppers, jalapeño peppers, okra, radishes, and we even tried watermelon. The jalapeño peppers were so hot! The longer they were on the vine, the hotter they became. One day Steve was picking them and didn't realize he needed gloves to handle the peppers. When he went to the house for a bathroom break, he scratched his balls and the skin burned like fire for two days! I laughed every time I thought about it.

I liked gardening, although it was a lot of work. When harvest time came, the work doubled, and I could barely keep up with the ripening bounty. I canned all the vegetables and even made my own ketchup. While I was out there sweating over the plants, Steve lazed in a lawn chair sunning himself, with our blue pedestal fan plugged into an outlet on the deck and placed next to his chair so he'd always have a cool breeze blowing on him. Once in a while he'd raise his head to give me a smile full of mischief and say "Hey Peep, your row's crooked." If anybody came over to visit, he'd tell them "It wears me out just watching her work."

By early September the money ran out, and Steve still wasn't working. He didn't collect unemployment. He could have, but he was too proud to be seen down at the unemployment office, and besides, he hated to stand in lines. As our finances grew more desperate, I began to write checks on one credit card to pay the other and just kept juggling them back and forth. With the produce from the garden we figured we could eat on a dollar a day.

In late September, Steve finally went back to work. He found a job with Van Epoch, a van conversion company, and he traveled to Lansing during the week to set up new accounts. Suddenly his income dwindled to half of what it was when he worked as a sales manager for Champion, and it hit him hard when he realized this was the best he could do for now. He'd loved his old job with Champion, loved their products, loved the sales people and the professional status he'd enjoyed there. When he was fired he went into shock, and now that he'd finally found work with Van Epoch, it only underscored the fact that he'd lost the job he really loved and would never be able to go back.

A few weeks later Steve met up with Perry, an old running buddy he used to know from the late sixties. Perry managed Curtis Ford now, a dealership in Lansing, and it was easy for Steve to sell him a few vans. Steve began drinking with him until all hours of the morning, and spending nights away from home with no word to me about his plans. If he wanted to stay at a motel when he'd had too much to drink, that was fine with me, but it drove me crazy when he didn't call to let me know he was all right.

The biggest shock arrived when he came home one night to tell me he wanted a divorce. He was completely sober, and the cool, rational tone of his voice made my blood freeze. At forty-three, he was sure he was doomed to a downward spiral and he said he didn't want to take me down with him. What he thought I was going to do without him, I have no idea. I was twenty-seven years old, and Steve had been the center of my life ever since I'd turned eighteen.

I tried to ignore this kind of talk, but it shook me to the core. Most days we barely said twenty words to each other. These last few weeks had been the most uncomfortable time we had ever spent together, and I was heartsick over it.

Tonight would be different, though. This morning I'd told him I was making the All-American Dinner, and Steve had brightened a little and promised he'd be home by six o'clock.

"You swear?" I asked as he got dressed for work. He looked so handsome in his suit and tie, and he smelled wonderful.

"Swear," he said, and kissed the tip of my nose.

Usually he kept his promises when I pushed him, and I'd pushed him hard. Over breakfast I reminded him how much he loved the taste of creamed corn, fresh from the garden, poured over my homemade biscuits.

"Six o'clock," I said again. "Not a minute later."

"Mm," he said.

"You'll remember, won't you buddy?"

He gave me a look. "I said I'd be here. I'll be here."

He watched me begin to peel the apples for pie, and the kitchen filled with their sweet, fresh fragrance. He knew how much work it was to get the All-American Dinner on the table while the food was hot and cooked to perfection. And he knew how good it would be.

Around five that afternoon I pulled out my old green electric skillet, its Teflon coating nearly scraped off because of use and abuse, and I placed it on the countertop, plugged it in and waited for the pan to heat up. Then I spooned a big chunk of Crisco into it and listened to the fat sizzle when it hit the hot metal. Steve butchered chickens when he was younger and his theory was that smaller chickens were better. I always bought a whole chicken, two or three pounds at the most. I tipped some flour from the canister I kept on the counter into a paper bag, added salt and pepper and threw in the chicken parts and shook the bag until the chicken was coated with the flour mixture. When the Crisco was hot enough I'd add the chicken, sprinkle a little paprika on it and brown both sides before I put the lid on and let it cook until the chicken was done. I'd take the lid off during the last bit of cooking, so the chicken would crisp up well.

Our dogs lined up around my ankles with an expectant look on every little face. We had five Chihuahuas by now: Charlie, Shelley, Sandy, Tessy, and Candy, and once in a while they'd bounce from one end of the kitchen to the other, toenails clicking and skittering across the linoleum, bodies wriggling in anticipation, just to let me know they were deeply interested in what I was doing.

Four golden Yukon potatoes sat scrubbed and waiting on the counter. I'd dug them up from the garden that morning, and now I paused to admire them. Why was a homegrown potato so much better than store bought? There was no comparison in taste. With a few strokes of the paring knife I peeled them, cut them into chunks, and tossed them into a pot of bubbling water.

While the chicken sizzled in the skillet I husked six ears of corn I'd picked from the garden and cleaned all the silk from the ears. One by one, I cut the corn off each cob and then scraped the cob with a knife to remove the juice and pulp. A half stick of butter was already melting in a pan on the stove, and I tossed in the corn and scrapings with a couple tablespoons of water, a teaspoon of sugar and a couple pinches of salt. Then I added cornstarch and water. I never measured, but I knew exactly how much to stir into the corn with a dollop of half-and-half. Presto, cream style corn.

Another five minutes and the potatoes were done. I drained the water from the pot, added butter to the boiled chunks of potato and mashed them by hand, then used the electric mixer and streamed in a little milk until they were smooth and fluffy. More salt, a little pepper. My mouth watered at the fragrance, and I dipped a finger into the creamy white mound and tasted it. Perfect.

The whole kitchen smelled like apple pie by now. Most people used tart apples, but I used Red Delicious apples because Steve liked his pie a little sweeter. I had a big four-cup measuring cup and I filled it twice with chunks of peeled apples, then mixed them with flour, sugar, cinnamon and just a little nutmeg. I'd made this pie so many times, I never measured anything. Apples were in season now, and we'd already gone to the apple orchard for a couple of bushels. I'd spent the whole afternoon making a dozen pies, and except for the pie we'd eat tonight, the rest were already nested in the freezer for the winter months.

It was time to set the table, lay out the homemade strawberry preserves and take a quick shower so I'd be fresh for Steve as soon as he walked in the door.

Music, I thought. When he walked in the door I wanted music to float through the air like champagne bubbles to lift our spirits. We both liked "Total Eclipse of the Heart" by Bonnie Tyler, Bob Seger's "Shame on the Moon," and Donna Summer's "She Works Hard for the Money." Joe Cocker and Jennifer Warnes had a new hit called "Up Where We Belong," and if Steve started making good money again I wanted to buy it for our collection. As soon as I finished dressing I'd go downstairs and pick out a stack of records for the stereo.

After I dried myself off from the shower I took a bottle of Jontue cologne from the counter and sprayed it in the air, then waved the cloud of scent over my bare skin. I pulled on fresh underwear, a pair of jeans and a tight red T-shirt that Steve liked, and then I rushed downstairs to check on dinner.

By six o'clock the house was spotless and filled with delicious smells that were driving me wild with hunger. Steve would be here any minute. Usually we ate in front of the TV, but tonight we'd eat at the dining room table, with quilted placemats and cloth napkins, and if Steve wanted to feed the dogs from his fingers while we sat at the table I swore I'd let it go. I wouldn't nag him or scold him or say anything about it.

I paced the house, straightened the place mats, swept the kitchen and checked my reflection one more time.

I knew it was a bad idea to watch the clock, but I couldn't help myself. *Six-thirty. Where was he?*

It's okay, I told myself. *He may have stopped off for just one drink. Let it go. Think about something else.* I put the chicken in the oven to keep it warm, but it didn't look nearly as appetizing as it did when it came out of the skillet. The biscuits were done, and I knew they'd turn into brown hockey pucks if I kept them in the oven, so I pulled them out and covered them up with a kitchen towel. The creamed corn had developed a skin over it, but I could still resurrect it with a little stirring and some fresh heat.

An hour passed slowly by as I drifted from the kitchen to the living room to the dining room and back to the kitchen, waiting, waiting, waiting for Steve.

Daylight turned to dusk, and dusk turned to black darkness.

The week before I'd started to hook a rug from a kit, and I tried to pass the time by knotting a few strands of yarn in the mesh underlay, but my heart wasn't in it. Each time a passing car cast its headlight beams into the window, I jumped up from the couch, pulled the curtain aside and pressed my nose to the glass.

Was it him?

No.

At eight-thirty I opened the oven and pulled out the chicken. It smelled greasy now, the skin dark and tough from overheating. The potatoes were cold. Everything looked dry, as forgotten and abandoned as I felt. A tight knot formed in my chest as I cleared the table, opened the refrigerator and shoved the plate of chicken inside, along with the corn, potatoes, biscuits, strawberry preserves and apple pie. I had no appetite. As I jammed the food in the fridge I swore I'd never make the All-American Dinner again.

The hours passed, and a cold rage welled up in me as I waited. *Rat-bastard!* If he dared to come home after all my worry and wasted effort, I'd chuck every piece of chicken in the garbage as soon as I heard his car in the drive. He wouldn't get to eat a single bite. Then I'd run upstairs and pretend to be asleep, so he'd never know how much I wanted him to come home. I could feel my stomach drop as I realized what a fool I'd been to believe him when he said he'd come home right after work.

Midnight came and went, and anger turned to anxiety as the hours crawled by. *What if he's lying in a ditch somewhere? Or unconscious in the hospital? Or dead?*

My legs ached from pacing the floor. *Why wasn't he here? He promised! He knew I was making chicken! How could he do this to me?* I sat down and plucked anxiously at the pillows on the couch, too heartbroken and exhausted to go to sleep.

Would he ever come home? What if he really wanted a divorce? What would I do if he'd left me already, and I was too dumb to realize it?

Sometime around dawn I finally dozed off and woke up a few hours later with my face pressed against the couch cushion. Saturday morning had finally come. I could tell it was around eight or nine because the sun streamed through the front window. The house ticked in the deep silence, and the quiet seemed unbearable. Before I could lose my nerve I crossed the room to the telephone, picked up the receiver and dialed the motel Steve usually stayed at in Lansing.

"Best Western," a voice said.

"Could you please connect me to Stephen Milks' room?" My voice trembled. Up until this moment it had been my longstanding rule to never call my husband when he stayed out late. I knew there was no point in arguing with a man who was drunk and didn't want to come home. When Steph and Stevie stayed with us in Canastota, I'd always refused to call Club 44 to talk to him, even if the kids pressured me to convince him to come home. I wouldn't beg, I told them. But I was ready to beg now.

Please let him be there. Please let him be alive. Please, Please. Please dear God let him be all right.

"Hello?"

It was a woman's voice. Graveled with sleep, breathy and low and sexy.

I covered my mouth with my hand and hung up the phone. My face burned with embarrassment. *Who was she? How long had he been with her?* I imagined her in a sexy negligee, her breasts pressed up against Steve's back in a motel bed, the two of them coiled together like snakes.

A burst of adrenalin flooded my limbs, and I ran upstairs to put as much distance as possible between me and the phone. The dogs barked and eddied around my feet and nearly tripped me on the stairs.

That goddamned cheating lying son of a bitch, I thought.

I yanked open the closet, pulled out my suitcase, snapped it open and left it yawning on the floor while I hurled armfuls of shirts, pants, jeans, sweaters and underwear into it.

How could he do this to me? I couldn't believe I'd prayed for him to be alive. He was alive, all right, and he was fucking somebody else.

Tears sprang to my eyes and streamed down my face as I slammed the suitcase shut, scooped it up and staggered downstairs. The overwhelming need to run away as far and fast as I could go swept over me, and I began throwing my things in a pile next to the door to the garage. Coats, dog food, purse, shoes, boots, and blankets. The pile of odds and ends grew as I blazed through the house and snatched up anything that caught my eye.

I never kept much cash in my purse, but after I went through drawers and counted out the change from the jar we kept in the kitchen, I came up with a little over fifty dollars. In a frenzy by now, I flung open the door to the garage, popped the trunk of the Electra and heaved the suitcase inside, then ran back into the house and lugged the pile of my belongings out to the car, one big armful at a time. I ran back inside, took my Pillsbury Cookbook out of the kitchen cabinet, picked up a fistful of silver from the drawer, grabbed a few pots and pans, whistled for the dogs and stomped back out to the garage.

Where do you think you're going? The voice in my head was coldly rational, and sounded just like my mother.

"We'll drive to Wisconsin," I said out loud. Steve's sister Susie lived in Wisconsin, about seven hours away, and if I didn't make a lot of stops the dogs could probably make it that long without a pee break. Susie and I had become close over the last couple of years, and I knew she'd take me in, no questions asked. Well, there would be questions, but she'd let me stay there for a while until I figured out what to do with the rest of my life.

I was terrified. Flat-out panicked, and my heart was beating so fast it felt like it was about to leap out of my chest.

I was scared to drive to Wisconsin.

Scared the Electra would break down and then what would I do with five dogs, stranded on the edge of the highway?

Scared that Steve was having an affair and if I did leave he would have no reason to come home.

Scared I wasn't strong enough to actually leave him.

The dogs yipped and whined and cowered at my feet as I scooped them up and forced them into the car. I had never traveled by myself with all five of the dogs—they weren't all leash trained and I wasn't sure what to do about that. My heart pounded away at my ribs as if it were trying to hammer its way out of my body.

Keys, I thought, *I need the fucking car keys and then I am Out Of Here. Goodbye Steve you goddamned cheating rat bastard son of a bitch.*

I darted back into the house, picked up the keys, raced out the door and let it slam behind me. In two seconds I was in the car with the key in the ignition and the motor running.

The Electra was eight years old now, and she needed a little time to warm up on cold mornings or she'd stall before I left the driveway. I sat in the driver's seat, torn between the urge to flee and the fear of what would happen when I finally rolled out of town and hit the interstate. The radiator had been leaking all summer, and I'd bought so much Stop Leak I should have owned stock in the company.

Would the car make it to Wisconsin?

I didn't know.

If I had car trouble, what would I do with five dogs? It had become a family joke that I hated to stop for gas, and I'd run out twice before. Both times I called Steve. What would I do when I couldn't call Steve to come quick and bail me out of trouble? I could picture us stranded on the side of the highway, with smoke billowing from the engine. Five dogs in the car, and all of us petrified.

Face it, the voice insisted. *You'll never make it to the Wisconsin border.*

I looked around at the heaps of clothing and pots and pans that cluttered the car seats. The dogs eyed me nervously, as if I were a stranger. Candy, my oldest dog, suddenly hunched over and vomited all over the seat.

"It's okay, baby." She huddled into a tight ball of misery while I stroked her fur and sopped up the bile with a couple of used tissues from my purse.

I took her into my lap, and tried to banish the thought of how sweet Steve had been with her when she was a puppy. He'd always been good with Candy, and she loved him so much.

What if … what if Steve wasn't in that motel room? What if that woman was the maid? Okay, she didn't sound like the maid, but what if she were a stranger who had just rented the room? What if the clerk was so used to Steve being in that room that the clerk transferred me without thinking, and the woman who answered wasn't Steve's mistress?

My breathing slowed, and suddenly I felt worn out. The fact was, I didn't know who that woman was. Maybe I'd never know.

That thought made the misery turn cold in my chest, and my heart ached with it. Tears stung my eyes as I struggled to wrap my mind around the fact that my marriage might be over. Steve had told me often enough in the past few weeks that he thought he should divorce me to save me from his own doom. Maybe he was right. Maybe he was already sleeping with someone else he liked better than me. We might never sleep with each other again. Useless tears filled my eyes, and I bent my head and cried in the driver's seat, my hands in a death grip on the steering wheel as if the Buick itself could comfort me.

I turned off the ignition, and the car went still. The engine ticked. The dogs quieted, their big brown eyes on me. I opened the car door and left it open as I walked back into the house with the dogs in a solemn procession behind me.

Steve would have to come home eventually. If he wanted a divorce, he'd have to tell me to my face, and then we'd talk it over.

Fuck it, I thought. I found a bottle of wine in the back of the refrigerator, uncorked it and poured myself a tumbler full.

For the rest of the morning, I drank one glass after another until the bottle was empty. It had been nearly twenty-four hours since I'd eaten anything, but I wasn't hungry—the thought of chicken and apple pie made my stomach churn. I opened another bottle, poured the purple liquid into my glass and sipped it slowly while the square of sunlight from the living room window moved across the rug and shrank to nothing as the morning fizzled into afternoon. Steve was still gone, gone, gone. I drank until the misery in my chest blurred and drifted out to my fingers and toes and floated off. Melancholy hovered over me, just above the surface of my skin, a dim gray shroud that clung to the furniture and tainted everything around me, but at least my heart no longer felt like it was being ripped in half.

What will I do if he never comes home? I asked myself.

Rough hands shook me awake. *Steve,* I thought, and gratitude poured through me. With my face down on the couch, I kept my eyes closed to savor the relief I felt at his touch, even though it seemed like he was shaking me really hard. I didn't want to wake up. For as long as possible, I wanted to postpone the conversation we'd have if he wanted to leave me.

"Peeps, wake up! Wake up! What happened?" His voice was loud, strained and upset.

I stirred, opened my eyes and stared at the phone receiver next to my face, and took in the phone upside down on the floor. *I must have called Susie,* I thought. I'd probably fallen asleep in the middle of our conversation. My cheek ached from being pressed against the couch cushions. My neck was stiff, but I didn't want to move yet.

Steve brushed the receiver aside and knelt on the floor next to me, his face pale, stricken, taut with anxiety. "Penny, are you all right? Can you hear me? Talk to me, god damn it! Penny!"

I blinked. He only called me Penny when he was dead serious or mad at me. It was like being called to the principal's office when he used my real name, but I couldn't remember what I'd done.

"Oh Jesus tell me you're all right," he whispered, and nuzzled my face. "Do you need an ambulance?"

My head ached from the sweet wine I'd been drinking all morning, and my tongue felt like a lump of suede, but why would he think I needed an ambulance?

I wiped my eyes with my fists and turned over on my back. "What are you talking about?"

He reared back on his heels. "The phone's been off the hook for hours! I've been trying to call you from work, and couldn't get through. Then I come home and find you lying here face down on the couch. What the hell happened?"

As I propped myself up on my elbow, the whole miserable night and day came flooding back to me, along with a sickening wave of nausea. "I'll tell you what the hell happened. I called your motel room in Lansing at nine o'clock this morning."

He studied me for a moment, his face impassive. "I wasn't there, was I?"

"They connected me to your room."

"They couldn't have. I didn't stay there last night."

"I asked for your room, they connected me, and a woman answered the phone. Who is she, Stephen?"

He looked genuinely puzzled. "How should I know? What did she tell you?"

"I hung up!" I said.

"Why didn't you ask to talk to me?"

"Because I didn't want to talk to you if you were in bed with another woman." My voice trembled, and my chest ached with grief. I hated to sound so weak in front of him. My head pounded with every furious beat of my heart. He reached for my hand, but I brushed it away.

He shook his head. "I told you, I wasn't there last night, Peep. Perry and I went out drinking after work and I crashed at another motel."

"I find that hard to believe." Suddenly I felt exhausted. At that point, I didn't know what to think.

"That's crazy! You're going to condemn me without a hearing?"

All I felt now was a crushing fatigue. The anger had fled, and I was so tired of feeling upset that I didn't have any energy left to argue with him.

I struggled to sit up. "It has to end, one way or the other. I can't do this again. Either you quit staying out all night, or one of us will have to leave."

He searched my eyes and nodded slowly, and his eyes seemed to turn a darker shade of blue as he studied my face. "I understand. I can see what all of this has done to you." He blinked and looked away. "When I walked in and saw you lying there, it just …" He shivered. "I couldn't stand it if I lost you, Peeps."

I took a deep breath and let it go. "If you don't give me the respect I deserve, you will."

His eyes filled with tears. "I'm done. No more all-nighters. I'll come home every night."

I wanted to believe him, but I'd heard his glib promises for nine years, and I knew he was capable of making bad decisions, especially when he was drinking. "I can't live through another night of wondering where you are, who you're with, whether you're dead or alive. You don't know what I went through, and if you had a scrap of respect or affection for me you would never torture me like that."

"I'll make this up to you," he said. "I don't know how, yet, but if it takes me the rest of my life, I swear I'll make it up to you."

He buried his face in my neck, and in spite of everything I touched his hair and began to cry. Why was I so scared of losing him? What power did he have over me that I couldn't stay angry with him? I loved this stupid man. I was stuck with him. I'd probably stay with Stephen Milks until death parted us, just like the judge said in the courthouse when we married each other. I was helpless to go against the strong river of feeling that flooded me now, even when I knew he could be lying to me every day of his life about where he'd been or who he was with. It just didn't matter. I buried my face in his hair and sobbed for all the hours I'd waited for him, sobbed for the two of us and the terrible confusion and pain of the past few weeks.

"Oh my sweet baby, I love you." Steve's voice broke. "When I saw you lying on the couch … Jesus, that scared me."

"You thought I tried to kill myself?" In spite of everything I laughed out loud. "Why on earth would you think that?" I'd never even thought of committing suicide, not once in my whole life.

"I'm sorry, Peeps." He hugged me so tightly I couldn't

breathe, and then held my face in his hands and stared at me as if he were holding a rare and precious treasure. "I know I've put you through hell these last few weeks, but I'll never spend another night away from you."

I closed my eyes. "You have to work. Of course you will."

"You know what I mean. No more all-nighters. No more crashing at a motel to sleep it off when I could be home in bed with you. I love you. I don't know what I'd do if you ever..." His voice trailed away and he squeezed me hard enough to make me cough, and then he loosened his arms and looked at me with a deep, sorrowful affection that brought a lump to my throat.

"I made the All-American Dinner," I told him. "You hungry?"

"Only for you," he said, and lifted me up in his arms.

∾ *Chapter Nine* ∾

The following spring it rained for ten days in a row, a steady, dreary April rain that made a lake out of the back yard, with clouds so low they covered the fields like a gray blanket and turned noon to twilight. I leaned back in my kitchen chair, stared out the window and pondered the dismal state of our finances. If I paid the electric bill with our MasterCard, paid the water bill with American Express, and used our Sunoco card for gas, would we have enough money in the bank to cover what we owed for rent? That afternoon I'd already spent twelve dollars in cash, and even though I came home with six grocery bags full of food, it hurt to dole out those twelve one dollar bills.

At this point in our marriage, Steve called me the coupon queen. I spent hours combing through the grocery ads, found items on sale and matched coupons to the sale items. It had taken me all afternoon to drive around town and coordinate the coupons with our stores. Meijers had a special to triple the value of the coupons, Walgreens had a promotion for toothpaste, mouthwash and deodorant, and A & P had a sale on chicken thighs at thirty-nine cents a pound.

I did not want to drive all the way to Detroit again to try and pick up Steve's check from Van Epoch headquarters. Last week I'd made the drive for nothing—the owners had shrugged and said they didn't have the money to pay him. The week before that, his paycheck bounced. Those idiots had no idea how to run the business efficiently, and Steve and I knew it was just a matter of time before the job would evaporate.

I heard the garage door hum as it opened, and the Electra's engine gave one last rattle and cough before it died. *How will we ever afford a tune-up if Steve doesn't get paid?* A minute later the kitchen door swung open, and when he walked in my heart relaxed at the sight of him.

"How's the Peeps?" He sounded hale and hearty, always the salesman, even when I was his only audience.

"We're broke," I told him.

He kissed the top of my head. "You'll figure it out. What do we have to snack on?"

I grinned in spite of myself. "Look inside the refrigerator."

Steve opened the fridge, stared at the shelves full of food and shook his head in disbelief. "You're a coupon genius. Pretty soon we'll be trading coupons for rent."

"I wish. Did they give you your paycheck?"

"They're working on it," he said. "They're having a dry spell."

"Steve, we can't go on like this—pretty soon we won't be able to pay our bills. We're going to have to come up with another way to make money."

He leaned against the kitchen sink and stared at the gray veil of rain beyond the window. "You know what we have to do."

"I'm all ears."

He turned around to lock his eyes on mine, and he spoke in the same confident, quiet and reassuring voice he used when he wanted to close a sale. "It's time to make The Fan."

This again, I thought. He'd been talking about The Fan for weeks now. When Steve first told me about his idea for a better ventilation system for RV's, I listened intently, and it did sound like a plausible idea. I just figured he would have dropped it by now.

He was always coming up with wild ideas to make money. Back when Steve was working for Champion, his boss Dave Struck found an apartment four-plex in downtown Flint that he wanted to buy, and he talked us into investing in it. We didn't have any money, so we borrowed ten thousand dollars from Buck's mother-in-law at fifteen percent interest. Steve and I worked on the apartments all summer, put in new kitchens, remodeled the bathrooms, laid new carpet and painted each apartment. Eventually we sold the apartments for a loss, and we were still paying off the interest on the ten thousand dollar loan.

That escapade made me wary of Steve's plans to get rich quick. I hated losing our hard-earned money on those apartments, and we couldn't afford to make another financial mistake. This real-estate failure didn't put a dent in Steve's optimism, though. In the past year he'd talked about buying a hotel, or a bar with pool tables, and then he'd been fired up about entering the touch-less car wash business.

All winter long he'd come up with one new whim after another. All of them meant going into debt. He had no problem picturing himself at the helm of a dozen odd businesses, but this fan obsession had become the main topic of conversation lately.

He slipped off his jacket, loosened his tie, unbuttoned his cuffs and rolled up his sleeves. The man did have beautiful arms. Something deep in my belly fluttered whenever I saw the plump swell of his biceps, the muscled curve of his forearms and those capable hands. He sat in the chair next to me and took my hand in his while the rain pelted against the window.

"We can do it, Peeps. If we don't, somebody else will. It's a great idea just waiting to happen, and whoever jumps on it is going to be rich."

I leaned back in my chair and tapped my pen on the checkbook. "How will we support ourselves while we start a new business? We've been living on credit cards since Christmas. We have no capital, no savings, no assets. Who's going to fund something like that? Santa Claus?"

He pushed his chair back and stood up. "We'll form a company, get some people to buy shares and use their money to start the business."

Let him talk, I thought. *Maybe he'll get it out of his system.*

Steve opened the freezer and peered inside. "Do we have any apple pies left? I could use some apple pie tonight."

"We ate the last one two weeks ago." I didn't have the heart to tell him we had chicken thighs roasting in the oven for dinner. Neither of us cared for chicken thighs, but they were too cheap to pass up, and they were better than the Ramen noodles we had the night before.

"Never mind." He sat down again, took a pen from his pocket and began to sketch the fan on a paper napkin. "I saw an automotive motor and fan blade today that I know would fit into the standard opening of an RV vent."

Here we go, I thought, and rolled my eyes. He could talk about The Fan for hours if I didn't stop him, with no thought to what this project might cost, or how to fund it, or how we could live without a steady paycheck.

"You know the problem with the standard RV roof vent … the hand crank for the dome is a bitch to turn, and it can skin your knuckles if you're not careful. The powered vents from Kool-A-Matic are so weak you could blow cigarette smoke straight into one, and fifteen seconds later you'd still see the smoke curling around the opening. It takes forever for those itty-bitty bathroom fans to move the air around."

I had to admit he had a point there. We'd traveled all over the country in demo RVs when he worked for Champion, and we both knew how hard it could be to get rid of cigarette smoke or cooking odors on a cold rainy night when you didn't want to open the windows. When Steve worked retail, he opened all the doors and windows in the RV's every morning to air them out for showing to customers. It was a fine system in the summer, but not so great when it was snowing outside.

Lightning lit up the horizon outside the window, and a long rolling boom of thunder shook the walls. I shivered as a fresh gust of rain spattered against the window like a handful of gravel tossed against glass.

Steve never looked up from his sketch on the napkin. "What I have in mind is something strong enough to give you a baby windstorm if you need it. Like an attic fan. It could have three speeds: low, medium and high. A turbine fan, with ten blades at a preset angle to really move air. All we need to do is design it to fit into the standard vent opening, so a buyer can pop out the old vent and put in our vent."

I pondered this for a few seconds while the rain pounded the roof. "If you put a hopped-up motor in there, wouldn't it be noisier?"

"The sound of the air being sucked out the vent would be the loudest thing you'd hear. Say you left your RV in the sun and it's hot enough to fry an egg on the dashboard. Wouldn't you want a fan that can move the hot air out of the vehicle as fast as possible?"

Steve waved his arms to illustrate the tornado of clean cool air, his whole body alive with conviction. Lightning cracked again, as if to emphasize his point.

I laughed in spite of myself. It was hard to imagine a sunny hot day while the storm raised a ruckus outside, but he always put on a good show when he was in the throes of an idea, and his enthusiasm was infectious. "You're really pumped about this, aren't you?"

"You said it yourself. We need to figure out another way to make money. Can you imagine if we had our own business, and we were both working on this? We'd be able to have a little conference whenever we wanted." He cut a sly look at me, grinned and wiggled his eyebrows in a highly suggestive manner.

I studied the curve of his arm, his elbow propped on the table, his fingers splayed out on the napkin as he went back to his sketch. When he came home at night it always felt like a push to cook dinner, eat dinner, feed the dogs, wash the dishes, dry the dishes, put them away, and by the time we both fell into bed we were exhausted. We might make love on weekends, but that was it.

But if he were here at one or two or three in the afternoon ...? Or ten in the morning? It would be wonderful to have him at home. To be able to hug him any time of day, whisper in his ear and nibble his cheek until he chased me up the stairs. To feel those strong arms lift me and bend me and open me up… oh yes. I could imagine that real well.

A tickle of excitement began to build inside me. If he were working at home, I could help him run the business. I'd be able to do more than hook rugs, weed the garden, can vegetables and bake pies. Just being around Steve during the day would make me happy. I missed him when he was gone all day, missed him with a hard ache that only lifted when he walked in the front door. Every time I saw him enter a room, I lit up, and no one could make me laugh like he did. So far in our marriage I'd spent most of my days alone, and I was sick of it.

Steve nudged me with his elbow. "You took all those business courses in high school. You're good with money, you know you are. You could do the paperwork. Pay the bills, chart a budget, keep the receipts straight. Hell, you've been doing that all along. You keep me on a damn allowance. You were made for this, Peep! Come on, let's give it a shot."

What have we got to lose? I thought. Even if we failed, it couldn't be any worse than his job with Van Epoch.

Steve was still talking, his eyes dancing with enthusiasm. "We could use better materials to make the fans, with higher quality plastic to stand up to outdoor conditions. Standard vent caps are so cheap they'll crack if a tree branch hits 'em. The sun beats down on that plastic and after a few years the dome turns cloudy."

"If we use better plastic, won't it be more expensive?"

"Maybe. Probably. I'm not saying it wouldn't be an uphill battle. We'd have to show the buyers that our fan would purr like a kitten and give them a strong summer breeze. It might be more expensive, but it would be worth it. We could offer a lifetime guarantee!"

It was wonderful to see him excited about something. All winter long he'd stood by his promise to come home every night, and he'd worked hard for a crappy salary with a terrible company week after week, month after month. I knew he was discouraged about the job with Van Epoch, and I didn't blame him.

He was still talking, reeling off facts and figures about how to move nine hundred cubic feet of air per second instead of two hundred and fifty. How he could build a prototype out of wood and take it to a tool and die shop to make the molds. How every RV owner in the country would want a better fan for the interior of his coach and would pay more to get it.

I nodded, smiled, and watched Steve work out the design in his head and draw it out on the paper napkin. Even now it made me smile to remember the sight of him stretched out on a lawn chair on our cement patio with that blue pedestal fan blowing on him. How many people would even think about using a fan outdoors like that? It was a great idea, too. Whenever I sunbathed I turned the fan on and it kept me cool and comfortable.

Steve went on talking about The Fan while I made dinner. He went on talking about The Fan while we ate dinner, cleared the table, and washed the dishes. For once in his life he volunteered to do what he called "women's work," and to commemorate this rare occasion I took a picture of him at the sink, up to his elbows in warm soapy water.

He never stopped talking about The Fan, and his enthusiasm was contagious.

Our own business! I wiped the kitchen table, straightened the place mats, and the more I thought about it, the more I smiled. *Why not?*

I put my arms around his waist, leaned my head against his back, and when he turned around to face me I kissed his nose. "Okay."

He eyed me cautiously. "You mean it?"

I gave him a squeeze. "Van Epoch hasn't paid you in three weeks. I'd say it's time we went into business for ourselves."

His eyes sparkled. "I'll quit that job tomorrow. Then we can start building the model."

Over the next few months he built a mock-up of The Fan out of wood. Every spare minute he had, he was out in the garage, sawing, scraping, chiseling, sculpting, cutting and gluing the wooden model. The Fan had several angles, curves and edges that were difficult to create in wood. His woodworking tools were limited, but he persevered. Weekdays, weekends and even on the Fourth of July, he slaved over the model for hours.

Without a blueprint for the model, Steve was flying by the seat of his pants. He built one prototype, scrapped it, started over and scrapped it again. The challenge was to create a model that would fit the standard roof vent opening, and incorporate the motor for The Fan—a flat pancake style motor with a shaft, the same automotive motor and fan blade he'd discovered back in April. This motor would be mounted on an H-bracket motor mount, with the fan blade mounted on the shaft of the motor and tightened with a set screw. After a dozen failures, lots of cursing and many nights of tossing and turning in bed, he finally came up with a wooden model for the base and the H-bracket that fit the automotive fan blade and motor perfectly.

When the wooden model was finished, he applied polyester fiberglass resin. The resin was mixed with a hardener and when the chemicals interacted the resin became hot and gave off a terrible smell. Thank God it was summer by then. After Steve stunk up the garage a few times he took the wooden model outdoors to the patio and applied the fiberglass mixture to the wood with a brush. Within a few hours the resin was hard enough to be sanded.

Sanding was my job. In addition to planting and weeding the garden that summer, I spent July and August turning the maple-colored model in my lap and sanding the bracket, corners and every surface with aluminum oxide sandpaper. Steve worked on projections of how many fans could be sold, which manufacturers might be interested, and how much money he thought we'd need to start producing them.

After I'd sanded the whole thing to Steve's satisfaction, he applied another coat of resin and I repeated the whole process of sanding. I'm not sure how many coats we applied. Most of the sanding had to be done by hand, because The Fan wasn't big enough for us to use an electric sander on it. Each edge and corner had to be perfectly rounded, and the dome had to fit precisely. It took months before the model looked the way Steve had envisioned it in his head.

When it was finally done, The Fan glowed with the warm butterscotch color of wood under multiple coats of resin, and the whole thing was smooth as satin. It was beautiful, almost like a piece of art, and we were both so proud.

Now we needed to figure out what to do with it.

Steve took the finished prototype to a tool and die shop to see how much it would cost for them to produce the four molds required to manufacture it. We needed molds for the dome, base, garnish (the interior trim around the fan) and the screen assembly, which housed the switches and the screen ring.

When he came home that night he looked exhausted. "The shop owner said he couldn't make the molds for less than a hundred and fifty grand."

"A hundred and fifty thousand *dollars*!?" I exclaimed.

Steve looked miserable. "I know. It's a lot more than I thought. I called around and tried to find someone who could do it cheaper, but they were all the same or higher."

He sagged on the couch, limp as a rag doll, his body still. Something in his posture sent a chill over my heart, but I didn't move. I didn't say a word. For a few moments I studied his face, alarmed to see the cobweb of lines that radiated from the corners of his eyes and creased his cheeks, lines that furrowed his brow and gave him a worried frown even when his eyes were closed. In the past year or so his hairline had receded, and I could see a new slackness around his jaw and neck. Suddenly he looked old. It shocked me to realize the cocky young stud I'd married had turned into a middle-aged man, and I hadn't even seen it until now.

As if he could hear my thoughts, his eyes opened and he glanced up at me. His face had always glowed with confidence, a confidence that bordered on arrogance, but now there was a hint of worry in his eyes, and it scared me. He was only forty-four. He'd poured his heart and soul into this project. Was all that work for nothing? It would break his spirit to start over, find a new job and go back to work for someone else. But how long could we go on pretending our idea would make us rich? For the past five months we'd been living on credit cards and food from the garden. What would we do this winter?

"What do we do now?" I asked.

Steve shook his head and let out a long sigh. "I don't know. I'll talk to Dave. He might have some ideas."

We were still friends with Dave, our old partner in the four-plex investment. Dave was the Vice President of Champion who originally hired Steve way back in 1975 as a salesman for their RVs. Dave had never liked the manager at Champion who had fired Steve, and didn't even know Steve had been fired until after the fact. Every few weeks Dave would invite us over for dinner, and he'd been keenly interested in our efforts to build a prototype of The Fan.

Steve and I had spent the last six or seven weeks trying to find a company that could build cheaper molds for us, with no luck—again and again, the bids came in at the same impossible figure: a hundred and fifty thousand dollars. In August and September he'd gone to all our local banks to apply for a loan, but when the banks found out we had no income and no real assets, they turned us down.

Dave lived in a condominium on McCandlish Road in Grand Blanc, which was one of the more affluent towns in our area. He spent a small fortune each year on his membership at Warwick Hills Country Club in Grand Blanc, where the Buick Open golf tournament was played. A true bachelor, he loved his vodka martinis, smoked cigars and cigarettes, and his condo was full of comfortable, masculine furniture. Golf trophies crowded the end tables next to the couch, and a string-art portrait of a yacht I'd made for him as a Christmas present hung on the living room wall. French doors off the kitchen led to a balcony where he kept his grill. His specialty was extra-thick grilled pork chops served with baked potatoes, salad and French bread, and after living on noodles all week, I was looking forward to dinner.

"Hey Struckie!" Steve called out as we entered the living room.

"I'm back here!" Dave sang out.

We found Dave at the kitchen counter, shaker in hand, raining salt on some pork chops arranged on a big blue platter. The fragrance of potatoes baking in the oven filled the kitchen, and my mouth started to water.

"You want me to set the table?" I opened the kitchen drawer where he kept the silver without waiting for an answer. This was my usual job whenever we came over for dinner, and as soon as I finished setting the table I would wash the lettuce, cut the tomatoes and cucumbers and mix up a salad dressing.

"No rush. Help yourself to a drink, have some crackers. I've got some good news," Dave said.

Steve poured us both a drink, sliced a piece of cheese, placed it on a cracker and offered it to me. "Good news? Man, we could use some of that."

"Oh it's good. It's very good." Dave grinned like the cat who ate the canary, and he let the silence bloom to make sure he had our full attention.

"Well?" Steve asked. "You going to tell us, or you want us

to beat it out of you?"

Dave spoke in a low voice, close to a whisper. "I was in the warehouse today at Champion."

"Yes …?" I said.

"I saw some molds," Dave said.

Steve and I exchanged a look, and suddenly our smiles matched Dave's.

"There they were, all heaped up in a corner. Four molds for a standard roof vent. The dome, base, garnish and screen assembly. I asked the foreman what they were going to do with them. He said Champion stopped building a vent, so the molds were obsolete and they were headed to the scrap yard."

"You're kidding," I whispered. *Holy baby Jesus, four molds that would cost us a hundred and fifty thousand dollars to replicate, and they were going to throw them out?*

Dave beamed at us. "So I asked if I could have them."

"No shit!" Steve was grinning like a jack-o-lantern by now. "Where are they?"

"Down in the garage. They're yours, if you want them."

For a second I thought Steve might cry. He grabbed Dave in a bear hug and they squeezed each other wordlessly, and then Steve let out a whoop and grabbed me and pressed me to his chest so hard I quit breathing, but I hugged him right back. We all clung to each other for a few seconds, then burst apart in an adrenaline-packed frenzy of talk.

"We'll have to get the molds re-tooled to fit my design—the base will need to have the H-bracket motor mount added. Maybe more steel reinforcement and support pillars," Steve said. "But re-tooling won't be anywhere near as expensive as making molds from scratch." His face shone with excitement. "You round up the investors and we'll split the ownership of the stock with you, fifty-fifty."

Dave nodded. "I know some people at the country club who would probably buy stock."

Stock? I thought. "What stock? We don't have any stock."

"We will," Steve said.

Their exuberance suddenly made me uneasy. The last time these two talked me into buying that apartment building, it had cost us a bundle. "How exactly is this going to work?"

"We're going to form a company," Dave said. "Get a lawyer to draw up the papers to create a corporation."

"What does that mean, create a corporation? Why do we need to be a corporation?"

"A corporation is like a real person—it can borrow money, lend money, pay its employees, do whatever it needs to do to conduct business. It's the corporation that will take the heat if we fail. We'll have limited liability."

"But we'll take other people's money?" *No way,* I thought. *Take money from strangers? Even worse, our families or friends?* "What if the company fails, then what? Wouldn't we owe them the money?"

Steve raked his fingers through his hair. "It's just like Vegas, Peep. You have to pay to play. People are going to want to bet on us, because they could win big. If they lose ..." He shrugged.

"Tell you what," Dave said. "I'll front you the money to buy your shares, and I'll buy an equal number of shares. Let's make it easy, price the shares at $100 each."

"We could offer a deal to anybody who buys shares before

Christmas," Steve said. "Give 'em a twenty percent discount."

"So we get a big pile of money, then what?" I asked. "We can't use it to buy food and gas and pay rent, can we?"

"We'll put the money in a business account," Steve said. "We'll use those funds to re-tool the molds, rent space to assemble the fans and ship them out, and hire people to work an assembly line. All that stuff. Whatever it takes to set up the business."

Dave nodded. "If everything goes well, in a couple of months Steve can draw a salary from the company. Then you'll have a steady paycheck."

"And until then?" I asked.

Dave shrugged. "You'll just have to live on credit cards."

My heart sank. We were already twelve thousand dollars in debt, and that debt weighed on me every night when I tried to go to sleep. That debt was the first thing I thought about every morning when I woke up and figured what coffee, eggs and bacon cost. Every time I sat down to pay bills it felt like I was digging our financial grave with my pen.

I leaned against the counter, my appetite gone, my stomach tight with dread. "How long will it take before Steve can draw a salary?"

Steve and Dave glanced at each other, and when Steve spoke his voice was soft, pleading. "Who knows? We have to take the gamble too."

Dave clapped me on the back. "What the hell. Somebody's going to get rich off this idea, so it might as well be us. Let's do it." He put out his hand, and Steve shook it.

For one delirious moment I was swept up in a feeling of

déjà vu, transported back in time to Club 44 with my hand on the poker pot, the keys to the Buick Electra slipping from my fingers as Steve gambled everything we had on the next card off the top of the deck. When he got that stubborn, happy look on his face I knew I was in trouble. He'd gamble everything we owned—and now, what other people owned—on his convictions. He loved to take a risk, and I hated it. He seized his dreams with a passionate abandon I'd never seen in anyone else. The greater the risk, the greater the rush, and the possibility of failure only made him happier.

It was why I loved him, and why I feared for us.

Most businesses fail in the first year, I thought. *If we go under, at least it will be quick.*

I swallowed hard. "Okay. I'm in."

"Fantastic!" Dave said.

Steve roared with laughter and lifted his glass of scotch. "Damn straight! Here's to Fan-Tastic Vent!"

∽ *Chapter Ten* ∾

In January 1985 we opened the business in the Soroc Plastics building on Dort Highway, right across the street from the showcase lot that Steve used to run for Champion. Every time I walked in the door, I felt a rush of elation. We were in business! Twenty-six hundred square feet on the front side of the building, and no, we couldn't really afford it, but we did it anyway. Now we had a big open warehouse to manufacture the fans, as well as two offices where we could answer phones, take orders and keep up with paperwork. My desk sat in the reception area, so I was the first person people would see when they walked in, while Steve had his desk in an adjoining office.

Dave loaned us $6500 to cover our share of the stock, and bought another $6500 worth of stock for himself. He still worked for Champion, so he wasn't actively involved in our company, but Steve agreed to give him fifty percent ownership, with the stipulation that Steve had the tie-breaking vote in any business decisions. Dave's investment gave us enough start-up money to rent space for the plant, buy used office and shop equipment, and purchase enough raw inventory to build a few fans.

Everything was so expensive, the money seemed to just disappear.

On my first morning in the new space, I sat behind my desk in my new office and felt overwhelmed by the task ahead of me: to devise a system to take orders, send the orders to the production line, and keep track of invoices for customers. If we wanted to make a go of it, we'd have to sell at least a couple hundred fans a month just to break even. That meant I'd have to keep all those bills and banking records straight, and I'd have to make sure the vendors who sold us all the parts and supplies were paid on time.

It had been ten years since I'd worked in an office, and the responsibility of setting up bookkeeping for our company gave me the jitters. I'd taken business courses in high school, but it felt like a lifetime ago. What if the IRS audited us? What if I failed to document the finances correctly? I was terrified of making a mistake.

Steve appeared in the doorway, walked over and tossed a check down in front of me. "Here you go, Peeps. Try not to spend it all in one place."

I studied the check. Five thousand dollars, payable to Fan-Tastic Vent. It was a personal check written with looping girlish handwriting and signed by someone named Carol.

"Where did this come from?" I asked. "Who's Carol?"

Steve gave me a wry smile. "Dave's cleaning lady."

The girl who cleaned Dave's condo was in her early twenties, and Dave had told us she was working her way through school by cleaning houses on the side. This was the first time a stranger wanted to buy stock in our company. What would Carol do if her gamble didn't pay off?

"This could be her life savings," I said.

He shrugged. "It's her decision."

We both stared at the check on the desk. My stomach

suddenly rippled with tension, and I shifted uneasily in my office chair. "It makes me nervous."

"We need the money, Peeps. Without people like Carol who want to take a risk on us, we'll never make it."

"I know," I said.

"The banks won't touch us," he said.

He was right. We'd approached a couple of banks for a small business loan, but when they realized we owned no property we could use as collateral, they turned us down flat.

"Take it," Steve insisted.

Hesitantly I picked up the check and held it in both hands. He and I never really talked about how we felt about selling stock in our company, but I'm sure it made us both nervous. Steve didn't ask his family or friends to buy stock, and neither did I— we didn't want them to lose their money if the company failed. In my mind, there was more than a fifty-fifty chance of failure.

"How's it going with the OEMs?" I asked. The original equipment manufacturers built RVs and sold them to the dealers, so the OEMs were our target market for The Fan. Steve had made dozens of calls to try and convince them that our fan would be a hit with the dealers.

He raked a hand through his hair and averted his eyes. "Here's the deal."

Whenever he said "here's the deal," I knew he was up to something. I put the check down on my desk and gave him my hard look, the one I used whenever I suspected he was trying to pull the wool over my eyes.

"Have you made *any* sales?"

He waved one hand in a dismissive gesture. "The OEMs

can't see past the bottom line. As soon as I tell them our price, they laugh in my face. They don't want to increase the cost of their product. We'll have to go in through the back door, straight to the people who live and travel in their RVs."

"How?"

His eyes widened the way they always did when he was about to make up some story to get me off his back. "Go to RV rallies. Do some presentations to the people who love RVs and use RVs and buy RVs. Show them how The Fan works better than the small roof vent fans. Let them create the demand with the manufacturers."

My stomach tightened another notch, like a cloth wrung tight. "That could take years! What do we do for cash in the meantime?"

"You're looking at it." He nodded toward the check in my hand.

"We're just going to go on selling stock? How long can we keep doing that if we're not making a profit?"

"Guess we'll find out." He shot me a grin, walked to the door and paused on the threshold. "Go ahead, take the check to the bank and pay some bills. Dave and I are meeting for lunch, so I'm off like a prom dress." And he was gone.

Four months later the business was $60,000 in debt, and we owed $25,000 on our credit cards. We'd worked day and night to sell a hundred and fifty fans, but we needed to sell five thousand to break even for the year. The only reason we were still in business was because we'd sold stock to some golf buddies and business associates of Dave's. That had brought in nearly a hundred thousand dollars. Unfortunately we'd spent all of that money, plus another sixty thousand dollars we didn't have.

Where did the money go? I asked myself that question every day. Our bills seemed enormous: we spent a fortune re-tooling the molds that Champion had given us—that took fifty thousand dollars right there—and then there were bills for materials, supplies, rent, utilities, and our payroll. In December, the company began paying Steve a small salary. Steve hired Jack Hartel to set up production—Jack had worked for Steve at the TransVan plant, so Steve knew he was a great worker and could get things done. In March we hired Steve's brother Buck to work on the assembly line. All these decisions required a constant outflow of cash, and some days it felt like I had to write one check after another just to keep the business afloat.

Every morning I propped open the door to the production area so I could see the assembly line Jack had set up in the next room. I wanted to know every detail of what was going on: how the fans were constructed, how they were boxed and how they were shipped. The assembly line wasn't anything elaborate—we had two tables for wiring switches and soldering screen cloth to the screen assembly, and a couple of stations for assembling the fans. There was still so much unused space that the walls echoed, and the room seemed almost empty.

One Saturday we drove to the plant in hopes of finding a check in the mailbox from a company that owed us almost two thousand dollars for fans they'd already received. Another company owed us eight hundred dollars. If they didn't pay us, we wouldn't have the money we needed to pay our vendors for the materials we'd already used.

Steve pulled the mail from our box, peered around the interior and wiped the floor of the box with his hand.

"Nothing?" I asked.

He shook his head. "Peep, we'll figure something out."

"We can't just wait around for these companies to pay us. You need to call them. Find out when they plan to pay us."

He snorted. "I can't call them. I'm the one selling them fans. I want them to cheer up when they hear the sound of my voice. If they connect my voice to the bill collector, our sales will go down the tubes."

"So what do we do?"

Steve held my gaze for a long moment. "You'll have to make the calls."

My expression must have changed because he smiled. "Come on, it won't be that bad. You can do it. I've seen you handle the phone. You're good at it."

Oh, I hated to take on that job. I was so shy I barely talked to anyone but Steve, Dave and Jack, and the thought of calling our customers to ask them to pay us made me cringe. But if I didn't do it, who would?

The following Monday I called our biggest account and asked to speak to their finance manager. My palms were so slippery with sweat that I nearly dropped the phone.

"This is Boyd." The manager's voice was clipped. Not a friendly voice at all.

"Good morning, Boyd. This is Penny, from Fan-Tastic Vent." My voice was hardly more than a whisper, my mouth was dry and my tongue stuck to the roof of my mouth.

"Yes?" Pages rustled in the background. Was he reading?

Signing papers? He sounded impatient.

I cleared my throat. "We shipped eighteen fans to you in April, and we haven't received payment yet." *What was wrong with my voice?* It vibrated with nerves, and I couldn't seem to steady it. I clutched the phone with both hands and stifled the impulse to hang up.

"April? Are you sure?"

"Yes," I squeaked. "We received delivery confirmation, and you assured us you'd send payment within a week. That was four weeks ago."

"Huh," he said. No apology, no effort to reassure me. "What's the P.O. number?"

"P.O. 14532."

"How was it shipped?"

"UPS."

He sighed. "Can you hold?"

"Of course." My face felt like it was on fire, and my whole body was rigid with embarrassment. I'd never had to ask a stranger for money before. Way back in the dark ages when I worked for a living at the RV lot, I never had to ask my boss for a paycheck. Now my gut twisted with tension as I listened to the silence on the other end of the line and waited for what felt like hours for Boyd to get back to me.

Suddenly the line crackled to life. "Hello? You still there?"

"I'm still here."

"I just signed the check, and I'll get it out in today's mail. Sorry about that."

He sounded breezy, almost flippant. Not sorry at all, but I didn't care. "Thank you so much!" I gushed into the receiver.

As soon as I hung up the phone I pumped my fist in the air and hopped around my desk in a happy victory dance. I felt like I'd just run a hundred yards for a touchdown. Unless Boyd was a big fat liar, we'd have a check in our mailbox by Friday.

On Memorial Day weekend in 1985, Steve and I drove to Marshall, Michigan to demonstrate our fan at the Glass Rally. At long last we would put Steve's theory to the test and see what the real RV owners thought of our product. We had stacks of boxed fans with us, and we hoped to sell fans directly to the people who owned RVs. What did we have to lose? Sales were so weak we had to do something or we'd go bankrupt.

The Glass Rally offered motor home owners a chance to get together for four nights of camping, musical entertainment, snacks, seminars, craft projects and classes. At least fifty vendors of products for the RV lifestyle were there, and hundreds of RV owners from around the country would attend the rally.

By the time we set up our booth, the fairgrounds were already bustling with people, even though it was still an hour before the booths were supposed to open. Steve and I lifted our four-by-six table and shifted it a few inches to keep it clear of the center aisle in the big barn-like space where the vendors had set up their wares. Our booth was nowhere near as fancy as the other booths, and we both felt a little intimidated by the slick displays we saw all around us. One vendor across from us sold chamois cloths, brushes, wipers and other tools for cleaning RV exteriors. Other vendors sold pots and pans, kitchen gadgets, jewelry, monogrammed shirts, hats, sweatshirts, and all sorts of tools.

Steve stared at the vendor next to us. They were selling TV antennas for RVs, and their booth had banners, a thick red carpet, tables with full color brochures fanned out on top of them, fancy lights and glossy pictures on easels. It looked like a palace next to our booth. All we had was a four-by-six foot table and a little wooden display for The Fan.

"I should have brought some carpet," I said.

"We'll know next time." Steve placed The Fan on the wooden display that he'd made and hooked it to a twelve-volt battery charger, so we could demonstrate how it worked.

My palms were already slick with sweat, and I could feel drops of perspiration rolling down my sides to my waist. It was hard to take a deep breath with so many butterflies in my chest. My whole body seemed to hum with the free-floating adrenaline of all the other vendors in the building, as well as the rising panic I felt at the prospect of talking to strangers.

"How do I look?" Steve dusted off his sleeves and rolled up the cuffs of his tailored white shirt.

At forty-four, he was still gorgeous. Not just to me—I'd seen him turn the heads of quite a few women, and back when he was working for Champion, I hated the way other saleswomen used to look at him. A few frown lines, a fine web of crow's feet, and a little more gray in his beard had appeared in the past year, and there were sun spots on his tanned skin. His hair wasn't as thick as it used to be. But he still had the bluest eyes I'd ever seen, a blue that changed color like the ocean, depending on his mood. He had broad shoulders for his height, a fairly narrow waist and a tiny butt. I loved that perfect little butt. Whenever he walked into my office, I'd look him up and down and he'd give me a smile because he knew what I was thinking. Just looking at him turned me on, and it didn't take much to set me off. A wink. A smile. Even the sound of his key in the door aroused me. Almost every night this week I'd woken in the wee hours of the morning in a fever of lust, and when I reached out to touch him, he drew me close for an early morning romp that left me breathless.

I raised my eyebrows at him, once, twice, and grinned. "I'd do you."

He burst out laughing. "I'd let you."

The loudspeaker crackled, and a recorded version of the Star Spangled Banner blasted through the building while the vendors went on with their frantic preparations. An announcer's voice welcomed all the attendees to the 1985 Glass Rally. Steve stood up straight and looked eagerly toward the doors, where a crowd of people pushed through and began to circulate through the aisles.

The first few people wandered by our booth, swept their eyes over The Fan and moved on without stopping. But they stopped at the next booth, where the salesman handed out brochures, and a knot of people formed around him as he began his spiel.

"Hey!" Steve called out to a couple who strolled by us. "You want to see our new RV ventilation fan? It's Fan-Tastic!"

They gave us tight smiles, shook their heads and kept on walking.

I was mortified. I'd never had to sell anything before. I didn't know how Steve could stand the rejection, but he appeared completely unfazed. A flurry of people breezed by without even acknowledging his greeting, and my face burned for him. How did he do it? His smile never wavered. He turned toward the next group of passers-by, called out a big hello as though they were long-lost friends, and they appeared momentarily confused by his enthusiasm. Then those tight smiles went up like a stop light, and Steve and I watched as they passed us by and paused to listen to the salesman at the booth next door.

If only we had something to give them! A business card, or a brochure, or something.

We were so proud of The Fan itself that it just didn't occur to us that we'd have to use more sales materials. We had a product that was obviously better than the standard roof vent. Why wasn't anyone stopping?

I should have baked cookies, I thought.

"What you got there?" A lean woman with salt and pepper hair paused next to me, her eye on The Fan.

Steve was shaking hands with a young couple who had halted just long enough to give him a chance to start his spiel.

I had no choice. I had to talk to her, or she'd leave. "It's a fan."

My words were drowned out by the noise of the crowd and the megaphone-loud voice of the salesman in the booth next door.

She cupped her hand around her ear. "Sorry, I didn't hear you."

"A FAN!" It felt like I was shouting, but she nodded.

What the heck was it that Steve said to potential customers? He had a whole spiel, filled with jokes and smooth talk aimed at closing the deal, and I couldn't remember a single word of it.

She looked around as if she were getting ready to move along, and I knew I had to say something or I'd lose her.

My words came out in a rush. "The Fan-Tastic vent moves a hundred times as much air as the tiny vent fan in your RV, and you can pop out your old vent and put this one into the same opening."

She nodded again and stared at The Fan. "You got it hooked up?"

I opened the smoked dome, showed her the switch, and gestured for her to turn it on. The Fan instantly whirred to life. It was tilted on the wooden display so she could see both the top and the bottom, with the screen and switches fully visible.

She put her hand over the opening and felt how much air was pulled through the bottom screen and out the top. "Oh!" She looked surprised. "That is nice."

"Other powered vents have a four inch fan blade. This has a twelve inch fan blade."

She played with the switches, listened to the three different speeds, and as she cocked her head I felt a little flush of pride at how quietly the motor ran.

"It has a low amp draw, too. You can use it anytime, even when you're dry camping."

By now I knew that RVs had different appliances—the fan, microwave, stove and refrigerator— that ran off the battery when there was no electricity available. RV owners called that "dry camping" or "boondocking." Since batteries only had so many amps available, a low amp draw for The Fan meant you could use it any time without a big drain on the battery. It was one of our biggest selling points.

"How about installation?" she asked. "Can we do it ourselves?"

"It's pretty easy. Most RVs have twelve-volt lighting in the ceiling, so the wiring is usually close and easy to find. There are two wires coming out of the fan—all you need to do is hook up the black wire to the black, the white wire to the white. It's do-it-yourself friendly, and there are some basic instructions for installation and weatherproofing it in the box."

"My husband can figure that out." She smiled at me. "I like it. How much is it?"

"One hundred and seventy-nine dollars."

She reached into her handbag. "Will you take a check?"

"Yes ma'am!"

My first sale! I was astounded. A rush of happiness flooded through me, and I couldn't help but grin as I fumbled through a box of spare parts for the fan. *Where was the vinyl bag for bank deposits we'd brought? Where was that pad of blank receipts?* Finally I found what I needed, hastily filled out the bill of sale, added the tax and made sure she had a copy to keep for a receipt.

"Larry!" she called over to a man who'd been listening to our neighbor's spiel. "Come see what I bought!"

Half a dozen people straggled over to our booth along with Larry, and Steve launched into his sales talk.

By noon, our booth was swamped with people. Larry and Emily had spread the word, and every few minutes they reappeared with another group of RV owners. By mid-afternoon, people were standing in line to see how The Fan worked, and buyers stood in line to write me checks and hand over wads of cash. Time after time, I had to step up and talk to people, show them how The Fan worked, and take in money for one sale after another.

Steve's eyes glittered with excitement as he gave his pitch, and his gestures blazed with enthusiasm. He held a piece of paper a foot below the screen, then released the paper to show how The Fan sucked the paper right up to the screen. No other fan had the power to do that. The onlookers knew what he was offering them: Fresh air. A strong summer breeze. A baby windstorm, if they needed one. Anytime, anywhere. He waved his arms, cracked jokes, laughed and used his whole body to convince the crowd that they needed our product. People loved it.

But the true star of the show was The Fan. It was clear to everyone who saw it that this fan was better than any other ventilation system on the market, and no one appreciated fresh air more than the people who owned motor homes.

We'd been trudging toward this moment for over a year, and we'd gone deep into debt and spent every day working side by side to nurture our business. By now the financial struggle had become so familiar it felt like a permanent fixture of our lives together. We knew how to be poor. I knew how to juggle credit cards, cut coupons, grow our own food and scramble to make ends meet.

My love for Steve never wavered during any of our financial struggles. Even when he was fired from Champion and lay in bed for three days, I knew he would find a way to recover his confidence, and my love for him had grown even stronger in the past year. We'd developed a true partnership. Whenever I was feeling down about our prospects with the business, he pumped me up, and when he was dejected I did the same for him. While I may have had doubts about the business making it, I never doubted Steve.

Now I looked at the smiling faces that surrounded him and my heart expanded with relief. At long last, I knew this was going to work. As he gave his talk I studied his face, really looked at him and the intelligence that shone from his eyes, and a rush of admiration filled me. *This is my husband!* I thought. *He actually invented this amazing product.* When I looked at the faces in the crowd I knew he'd created something useful, something every RV owner would want.

Steve caught my eye and gave me a smile I felt all the way down my legs, and a great rising tide of loose and crazy happiness surged through me and lifted me to my tiptoes.

You are going to get lucky tonight, Mr. Milks, I thought. *And so am I.*

❧ *Chapter Eleven* ❧

By 1990, Winnebago, Fleetwood, Champion, Camping World and several other big names in RV sales and manufacturing offered our fan to their customers. We were flooded with orders. Sales were booming! Letters from grateful RV owners poured in, along with a steady stream of positive reports from industry journalists who raved about our invention. After a year of paperwork and nail-biting, our application for a patent on The Fan design was approved, which our attorney told us was rare, rare as getting struck by lightning.

Steve wasted no time in bringing the family on board to share our success, as well as the work of filling all those orders. We hired his son Stevie, who had grown into a handsome young man in his twenties, Steve's brother Larry and Larry's new wife Chris, Buck and his son Bucky, as well as Dorothy and her husband Jim, who both traveled to promote The Fan at rallies. Our friend Tom Jensen—another Champion man—came to work for us, as well as his wife Joanne. We also hired both of Jack's daughters. There was plenty of work to go around, and it was wonderful to walk in the doors of the business and see all those familiar faces.

The whole plant felt like an extended family, and our love of animals flowed from our house to the business. At any given moment, we had four or five dogs running around, and an African Grey parrot watched over all the comings and goings with interest. Our employees often went to Steve for advice, to hear his perspective on a subject, or to borrow money. He didn't pull any punches—if he didn't like their behavior, they knew it. He had no patience with whiners or slackers. When he was tired of listening to me or anyone else dither over a decision, he'd say "Handle it." That was one of his favorite expressions.

It still made me anxious to watch money fly out of our accounts to cover expenses and meet the payroll, and I couldn't quite escape the feeling that our success might vanish overnight. I'd been scrimping and saving and paying down our credit card debt for so long that I felt poor down to my bones. I never bought anything for myself—not even clothes. Steve used to yell at me to go out and buy something just for me, and when I stubbornly refused, he started buying me clothes for Christmas and my birthday. Whenever I went to the grocery store I still carried a purse full of coupons.

One Sunday afternoon Steve and I went shopping at Meijer Thrifty Acres, a grocery/department store we both liked. As usual, Steve grabbed a cart and launched it toward the aisles while I scurried to catch up with him, my hands full of coupons that I plucked from the envelope I always carried in my purse. He was going too fast for me to check out the specials posted on the windows at the front of the store. He pushed the cart through the aisles like a man on a mission, with no hesitation, no price checking, and no thought of menu planning. He casually tossed one item after another into the basket, things I would never have bought in a million years. Creamed herring. Name-brand bags of chips. Olives, pickled asparagus, and half a dozen other luxuries we didn't need.

When I saw him pick up a package of T-bone steaks and throw them in the basket, I stared at him in disbelief.

"We can't afford that, put it back."

He looked at me and laughed, his eyes twinkling. "We can afford it."

I gripped my envelope of coupons like it was the last life vest on the Titanic. "I've got two coupons for ground beef here. That's all we need."

"Come on, Peep. Let go a little. Put those damn coupons away and throw something in."

I hesitated.

Sure, things were good now, but how long would it last? So far we'd been lucky. What if that luck vanished? Debt seemed like a rising tide I had to battle night and day, just to keep it under control. If I bought any extras at all it was something for the house or Steve or the kids. That was how I stayed safe. This fear of spending drove Steve crazy, and until this moment he'd done all the splurging for both of us.

He held up a pound of name-brand bacon, flipped it into the basket and then picked up a big crown roast. He checked my face and laughed out loud at how shocked I must have looked. *Thunk!* The crown roast hit the other packages in the cart and tumbled to the bottom.

He gave me a sly look. "It's your turn. Throw something in."

He might as well have held out a hypodermic needle full of heroin and told me to shoot up.

How could I explain this churned up feeling inside? It was fear. That's all it was. I knew that, but it didn't make it any less scary to imagine throwing caution to the wind in a grocery store. I had a system. I knew how to save money, lots of money. All it required was a firm "no" whenever temptation stared at me. Who would say "no" if I began to say "yes?" What if this "yes" turned into a habit, and we slid down the long slick tunnel of temptation into bankruptcy?

Steve didn't wait for an answer. He strolled ahead of me as if he didn't have a care in the world, while I pushed the cart along behind him, afraid to raise my voice in the store but feeling even more desperate by now.

He lifted a package of Oscar Meyer bologna as he walked backward, facing me, and tilted it from side to side to taunt me. He knew I loved bologna sandwiches, but I never bought name-brand anything. I always chose the cheaper generic store brands.

"You know you want it," he crooned.

I rolled my eyes. "Give me that."

He passed the package of bologna to me.

My heartbeat quickened. Okay, it was over a dollar, but I knew it was really good bologna. It was darker than the pale generic bologna I usually bought, and I knew it tasted better. My mouth watered as I stared at it.

I swallowed hard, nestled the bologna into the child seat of the cart and kept it there, just in case I came to my senses and wanted to put it back. It was on probation, as far as I was concerned.

Steve stood in front of the cookies in the next aisle, picked up a package of Keebler's Fudge Striped shortbreads and held them up for my inspection.

"Mm-mm." He grinned at me, and I felt a warm glow right down to my crotch. He knew they were my favorite cookies, but I would never buy them for myself. Often on the way home from work, Steve would stop and buy me a package of Keebler Fudge Stripes, and when he walked in the door he'd sing out, "Peep, I've got a surprise for you."

He handed the package of cookies to me and I threw it in the basket. *What the hell,* I thought. *We can probably afford it, just this once.*

After that it was all over. The next aisle held dishtowels, regular towels, pot holders, and pots and pans. I picked up a plush white bath towel and threw it in the basket. Steve picked up three more and stacked them on top. He knew I had a weakness for good towels, but I'd never, ever bought anything but cheap, thin towels for us.

I began looking at the shelves to study packages I'd never dreamed of buying, and I imagined what it would feel like to reach out, grab them, take them home and try them out. Breck shampoo? *Why not?* Hazelnut flavored coffee? *Thunk!* It went in the cart. Haagen-Dazs chocolate chip ice cream? *Plop!* A whole pineapple, a bag of tangerines, honeydew melon? By the time we hit the produce aisle I was carrying armloads of fruit from the display case to the cart like a crazy woman. Steve laughed and flung in all sorts of things we'd never tried before: goose liver paté, caviar, dried apricots, French roasted almonds, and a fistful of expensive doggie chew toys.

When our cart was full to overflowing, Steve balanced a box of Russell Stover chocolates and a bouquet of roses on top of our loot, and we grinned at each other. I felt wild. All my good intentions, all my normal everyday scrimping scrounging vigilance had been blasted apart by this basket full of all my secret fantasies. As we pushed the cart to the line for the cashier, I felt flushed and embarrassed by the insane pile of goodies in our cart, but truthfully? I was happier than I'd felt in months, and I wasn't about to take anything back. I felt big. At long last I'd pushed past some cautious nagging part of myself that thought the world would end if I ever abandoned myself to the pleasure of buying what I really wanted.

When the cashier rang up the last item, Steve paid with cash. He loved having a wad of cash in his pocket, anything up to a couple of thousand dollars. A money clip was too small, and he'd switched to a rubber band to hold his walking-around bankroll. Everyone knew about the rubber band. That was just what was in his pocket—he kept even more in his wallet.

Until now Steve had been the big spender in our family, but I was finally willing to learn. I loved it. It was fun. And most of all, I loved running past the timid boundaries of my own life to scoop up whatever my heart desired.

What the hell, I thought. *Maybe anything is possible.*

That night Steve and I made love like animals, with a deep, thrusting, insatiable recklessness that mirrored the surrender I felt in the grocery store and teased the deepest part of my being into a frenzy of wanting. Wanting something, wanting more, wanting his body, his seed, a wanting that made me reach for him again and again until my flesh had been pounded sleek and open and I dissolved into him until there was no knowing where his skin began and mine ended. We fell asleep wrapped tightly in each other's arms.

I had a dream I was in a doctor's office. I was lying down on a table while Steve stood by my side and held my hand. The doctor explained that sometimes vasectomies reversed themselves if a couple had lots of sex and the woman was young and fertile. After all, I was only thirty-four, in the prime of my childbearing years. With his eyes half closed, the doctor ran his hand over my bare belly to feel the curve of my swollen flesh, as if he could see under the surface. In the dream his touch was soothing, almost erotic, and deeply reassuring. Then he looked deep into my eyes and told me I was carrying a boy. He assured me the baby was healthy. He said I would deliver the child in the fall.

When I woke up I felt an urgent, physical yearning, a deep tug in the center of my womb. I pressed my face into the pillow, clutched the sheets and pushed my whole body into the mattress. I wanted a baby so badly. More than money or success or anything we could buy at a grocery store, I wanted Steve's baby. Was the dream a sign?

I'm pregnant, I thought.

I flipped over on my back to savor the thought. This heaviness in my womb, this pleasant ache … what else could it be? The way Steve went after me night after night … didn't all that passion mean something? Didn't the universe want me to have a baby?

I'm going to have a child, I thought.

My whole body leaned toward the thought. *Who does our boy look like?* I wondered. *Would he have Steve's blue eyes? My dark hair? Whose nose? Whose mouth? Whose ears?*

I couldn't stop grinning at the idea of a baby, *our* baby, and

I stretched my arms overhead and thought about what a pleasure it would be to feel my belly swell with each passing month, to feel my little boy kick and push inside me with the nubs of his little fingers and toes. I couldn't wait to lean back against doorframes to make my bump more visible to others, and, oh yes I would go right on working until my due date, but I could just imagine Steve nagging me to sit down and put my feet up. That would be so much fun, to make him worry about me. Yes, I'd probably have swollen ankles and I didn't even want to think about the pain of childbirth and how my ribs would probably feel like a birdcage turning itself inside out when I finally had to let my boy leave my body and come into the world, but I'd have a baby! A son! A sweet darling creature with eyebrows like angel wisps, and eyes that were as blue as the ocean. His father's eyes.

My baby wasn't even the size of a cupcake yet, but I was already totally in love with him.

I wouldn't tell Steve. Not yet. He wouldn't understand. Back in my twenties, I went through a phase where I thought I was pregnant every time my period was late. I visualized what the baby would look like, whose features would be prominent, what we would name it. The bliss lasted until my period started and then I'd fall into a deep depression and cry for days. Steve was patient when I fell apart, reasoned with me about the vasectomy and how unlikely it was that I would ever become pregnant. He tried to joke about it. He sent me flowers every day, and he stayed at home with me as much as he could. There were times when he held me tightly and cried with me, not because he wanted a baby, but because he couldn't stand to see me hurt and sad. We talked about adoption, but it wasn't just the baby I wanted, it was the whole package: the pregnancy, the baby kicking inside me, the slow parade of months where my belly grew to a bulge that attracted strangers and made women envy me. I wanted all of it, even the pain and shock and glory of childbirth.

Back then I was jealous of every pregnant woman I knew. I didn't want to talk to them. I didn't want to have lunch with them and hear them complain about their morning sickness or stretch marks or weight gain. I wanted morning sickness. I wanted those stretch marks. I wanted to grow round and ripe and voluptuous, like them. I wanted a child.

Eventually I had to push the thought of having a baby to the back part of my brain, where I shut the door and locked it up as tightly as I could.

Until now.

I rolled over in bed to study Steve's face. *Please,* I prayed. *Let me have our son.*

A week later I woke to shooting pains in my lower abdomen, and a smear of red between my thighs. I rushed to the bathroom, sat on the toilet and felt blood pour out of me until the bowl filled with bright crimson.

No!

Even though I clamped my legs together, I couldn't stop the flow of blood. I lowered my face to my hands as the tears ran down through my fingers and dripped on my legs. The pain grew more intense, sharp enough to make me cry out.

What was going on with my body?

The bleeding went on and on and wouldn't stop.

Days went by, and still I bled.

I used up box after box of Kotex. One week after another, and another, and another, and I continued to bleed. When my period finally stopped, I started bleeding again a week later. I spent hours in the bathroom, doubled over in agony. Something was wrong, and I couldn't ignore the pain any more.

"You're going to the doctor," Steve said one night when he found me groaning on the toilet at three a.m.

"I don't want a doctor," I moaned.

"Peep, we need to figure this out. Something's wrong and I can't stand seeing you hurt like this."

I knew he was right, but I didn't want to go get prodded and poked by a doctor. Last time I felt pain like this was way back in 1974, right after I met Steve. Back then I spent a whole week in the hospital and they still couldn't make up their minds about what was wrong with me.

"Maybe it's just stress," I said.

"If it's stress, then the doctor will tell us, and we'll deal with it. You're making an appointment tomorrow."

The next day Steve talked to Dave, and Dave gave him the name of a specialist with good credentials who was willing to see me the following Friday. When it finally came time for the appointment, Steve went in with me for the exam.

Dr. Dale was in his mid-fifties, with salt and pepper hair and glasses, and he looked a lot like the doctor in my dream. After I undressed and lay on the table, he ran his hand over my abdomen, the same way the doctor had touched me in the dream. But this was no dream.

"Do you have prolonged or painful periods?" he asked.

I didn't want to admit anything. The silence went on until

Steve broke it.

"She does," he said.

"Sharp stabbing pains in your abdomen?"

I kept my lips tightly sealed. If I opened my mouth I knew I'd start crying, and I didn't want to cry in front of a stranger.

"Yes," Steve said.

My hands were sweating, even though the room was cold.

"It feels like you have a mass over your right ovary." Dr. Dale palpated a lump near my groin that had grown progressively larger and more painful over the last few weeks.

He went to the sink, turned on the faucet and washed his hands. "We'll need to do a laparoscopy to confirm, but I believe you have severe endometriosis."

"Okay," Steve said. "What's that?"

Dr. Dale dried his hands on a paper towel. "Endometriosis is the growth of cells similar to those that form inside the uterus, but in a location outside the uterus. When these cells attach themselves to tissue outside the uterus, they can cause trouble."

"How do we fix it?" Steve asked.

The doctor shrugged. "There's no cure."

His words hit me like a sledgehammer. *No cure.* I stared at the doctor, willed him to take it back, to un-say those words, or at least laugh and tell me he was joking.

He lifted his hands, palms open. "There are some treatments to alleviate the pain in mild cases of endometriosis. Sometimes it helps to block the menstrual cycle with hormones—that might ease pelvic pain." He glanced at Steve. "But your wife's endometrial growths are fairly large, especially over her right ovary. Hormones would bring only partial relief, if any, and of course the side effects can be severe."

He turned to face me. "You'll probably need a hysterectomy within a year."

My body froze. The word "hysterectomy" floated in the air between us like a knife. I didn't want to take it into me. I didn't want to feel it.

"You can think about this for a while," the doctor said. "We can put you on hormones, and see if that helps. But ultimately …" He shrugged once more.

My eyes filled with tears. This was my only choice? Unbearable pain, or the loss of my uterus?

I turned my face to the wall.

The surgery was scheduled for July of 1990.

The week before I was due to enter the hospital, I tried to keep busy. Summer was always a hectic time for us, and the phone rang non-stop. Jack's daughter Kim worked in the office with me, and we were always running to catch up. I figured the taxes for the payroll, made out one payroll in advance, wrote out all the paychecks by hand, typed invoices for our customers and filed carbon copies for our records.

The day before I was due to go to the hospital, I felt a free-floating anxiety I couldn't control. Panic rose up in me like a hurricane, and squeezed my lungs until I couldn't seem to take a deep breath. To take my mind off the surgery, I cleaned the house from top to bottom and made spaghetti sauce for Steve to heat up for dinner while I was gone.

The next morning I had to give myself a Betadine douche and wash myself with an antibacterial soap before we left for the hospital. My hands trembled as I mixed the solution, and the Betadine stained my crotch a deep, ugly yellow. Even though I scrubbed myself with the antibacterial soap, I couldn't get rid of the stain.

Finally Steve and I drove to the hospital in a tight, uneasy silence to check in for the procedure. Nothing looked real to me. Buildings, cars, trees—everything had a bright, sharp edge to it that hurt my eyes. My teeth buzzed, as if I'd drunk eight or nine cups of coffee.

At the front desk of the hospital, Steve filled out insurance forms at the front desk while a nurse led me to a room where she instructed me to change into a gown and stretch out on the hospital bed. The room was freezing cold, even though it was a hot summer day outside. After I undressed and changed into the thin cotton gown, I lay on the bed, stared at the fluorescent lights overhead and shivered like a dog.

A few minutes later she came back into the room with an electric razor to shave my pubic hair. While she framed the area with a sheet, I kept my face turned away. She asked me to spread my legs. The cold razor around my private parts felt so strange.

After she left I lifted the sheet to see what I looked like down there.

Steve walked in while I had the sheet raised and gave me an anxious glance. "You okay?"

I tilted my head. "You've got to see this."

He walked over, peeked under the cloth and flashed a smile at me, blue eyes twinkling. "Just like a newborn baby."

The nurse and an orderly appeared in the doorway with a gurney. "Mrs. Milks? Are you ready?"

My heart fluttered like a bird trapped in a cage. *Please dear God let me live through this, let it be easy, let it not hurt too much.* They rolled the gurney into the room until it was parallel to the bed. I sat up, pinched the hospital gown closed behind me with my fingers, then moved from the bed to the gurney.

Steve walked over to kiss my forehead, and I hugged him as tight as I could and whispered in his ear. "No matter what happens, I love you now and I'll love you forever."

He leaned toward my ear. "Peep, you're going to be just fine. I'll stay with you for as long as they let me."

The nurse took off my glasses, gave them to Steve and signaled the orderly to wheel me away, while Steve followed us to the pre-op area. In another icy cold room the nurse wiped my wrist with alcohol, probed my skin to find a vein for the IV, jabbed me with the needle and missed. She pulled it out to try again. After five or six tries with no success, my hand felt like it was on fire. Finally she smeared Lidocaine on my wrist to numb the skin. As she jabbed me again, my lips quivered with the need to cry.

Without my glasses, I couldn't see what she was doing. My mind buzzed like a swarm of bees. *She's hurting me! This isn't working! I don't think I should do this!*

A doctor I'd never met before breezed into the room, introduced himself and said my surgeon might not be able to make it, but we could go ahead without him.

By now I was shaking with rage as well as fear, and when I spoke my voice vibrated with anger. "If Dr. Dale doesn't show up, I'm not doing this."

The doctor exchanged a look with Steve, and they both

smothered a smile. I wanted to punch them both in the nose. The nurse stabbed me one more time with the needle, finally found a vein that would hold the IV, positioned the bag of saline next to the bed and hurried out of the room.

I glared at Steve, and he shifted uneasily to avoid any eye contact with me.

A few minutes later Dr. Dale appeared in the doorway, and as soon as he came over to greet me I clutched him by the sleeve of his lab coat.

"Have you ever had a patient not wake up from anesthesia?" I asked.

Steve rolled his eyes. "Peep, if you don't wake up, you'll never know. Quit worrying."

The doctor patted my arm. "No, Mrs. Milks. Every single one of my patients has woken up from anesthesia."

"And you're sure there's nothing else you can do to help the pain?"

"I'm afraid not. This is the only way."

Reluctantly I released his sleeve. It was too late to change my mind—I had to go through with it. I knew I had to let go, and I hated letting go. I swallowed hard, crossed my hands over my chest and closed my eyes.

"Okay, then," I whispered. "Let's do this thing."

Awareness bled through the fog. Slowly, slowly, feeling came back to my fingers and toes. I could hear someone whispering. Two people whispering. Nurses. Their voices made a soft shushing sound nearby, but I was so tired I couldn't open my eyes.

Poor thing, her heartbeat went up to a hundred and forty beats per minute during the surgery.

I bet Dr. Dale had a fit.

He freaked. Thought she was having a thyroid storm. Last week he had a patient die on the table because of a thyroid storm. He had to call in another surgeon to keep her stable.

Her husband is about to lose it out there. Wants to know what's happening and why it's taking so long.

No wonder! They told him it would only take forty-five minutes, and she was under for three hours. Shh, I think she's coming out of it.

The gurney jerked underneath me as one of the nurses started to wheel me down the hallway. My eyes fluttered open. I was still so drugged I couldn't talk, but a sharp pain seared the center of my body. It felt like someone had shaken out all my organs and replaced them with hot coals.

The pain grew even more intense after the nurse pushed the gurney into the elevator. As the numbing effect of the anesthetic faded, I felt more and more like I'd been stabbed in the belly and the knife was still in there.

When the elevator opened, I saw Steve pacing the hallway. As soon as he saw me he rushed over, bent down close to my face and kissed my forehead. He looked tired, his face lined with worry.

"How was it, Peep?" he whispered.

"It was a motherfucker."

He stroked my hair. "At least it's over now."

Resentment, fury and heartache boiled up in me all at the same time. *Yes, it's over,* I thought. *I will never have a baby now. I will never be a mom, and the child we might have had will never be born.*

"I'm going to buy another dog," I told him.

He laughed out loud. "Not if I have anything to say about it."

You don't, I thought. *Not this time.*

By now we only had one dog, Tessy, and she was getting old and stiff and just looking at her reminded me of my own pain. The first week out of the hospital, I walked around like a ninety-year old woman. It was impossible to straighten up—it hurt too much.

But my arms ached for a baby of my own to hold and love. As soon as I was able to drive, I went looking for a puppy and found a tiny black-and-tan miniature pincher. For me, it was love at first sight, but Steve wanted nothing to do with him. I named the puppy Corky Beau and I had my baby, for about three hours. As soon as Corky saw Steve stretched out on the couch, he curled up on Steve's shoulder and it was all over but the shouting. Steve fell in love, and my baby became his baby.

Whenever Steve had to leave town for a business trip after that, Corky dragged himself around the house as though he had no reason to live. His ears hung limp. His tail curved down and stayed there. He looked so pitiful it was almost funny, but we both longed for the moment when Steve would finally walk in the door. Then Corky wagged his tail so hard it shook his whole body, and he ran in tight, crazed circles around Steve's legs while we laughed. That dog was head over heels in love with my man.

How could I blame him? I knew exactly how he felt.

❧ Chapter Twelve ❧

By 1992, our lives were consumed by the business. Every morning, Steve and I drove to the plant to put in ten to twelve hours of work, and after we drove home at night we talked until we fell asleep about ways to improve the business. With every warranty card we received, Steve asked the customer if they had any suggestions about how we could make the product better. Our buyers loved the attention we gave to their needs, and the demand skyrocketed. We were overwhelmed with orders that streamed in from more than a hundred companies all over the world.

We needed help, so Steve hired relatives, friends, and friends of friends. We quickly outgrew the space on Dort Highway, and purchased a building in the nearby town of Capac, about twenty miles from Lapeer. When the business outgrew that space, we added twelve thousand square feet to the building. It was a beautiful space, a friendly space, and we loved going to work every morning in our pretty new building.

Steve and I had come a long way. We had forty-seven employees, our payroll was close to a million dollars a year and our own income rose steadily as the business expanded. Success soothed my financial anxiety, but I still kept the brakes firmly applied to Steve's desire to spend. That man always wanted to buy things: new equipment, cars, trucks, boats, land, businesses—

you name it, he wanted it. I had to hide the catalogues that came in the mail every day, or Steve would have spent every nickel we had. Whenever he asked me how much money we had in the bank, I'd make up a figure that was a good deal less than what we had in our savings account. He knew I would never tell him the real figure, and I knew he secretly liked this, even though he was always tugging at the purse strings. It made him feel secure to have enough saved for a rainy day.

When our Stevie told us he wanted to marry his girlfriend, and a few days later our Stephanie told us she'd found true love and wanted to get married, we were both thrilled for them—not only because they were finally going to settle down and build families of their own, but because Steve and I had plenty of money saved to see them married in style.

The first big event was Stevie's wedding to Angie in 1993. Steve bought round-trip plane tickets to Reno, Nevada for Stevie and his bride Angie, Stephanie and her fiancé Scott, and tickets for half a dozen friends and relatives as well. During the four-day wedding extravaganza in Reno, we paid for motel rooms, several golf outings and the wedding dinner.

Wherever we went that weekend, Steve peeled bills off his roll to pre-tip every waiter and waitress who served us. If he liked the band, he paid them to play longer. If he was on a winning streak at blackjack while the band was playing, he peeled bills off his roll to make sure they went on playing all night.

Our first night in the hotel, we lay in bed together whispering, giggling and re-living our favorite moments of the day. Steve stretched out on the bed, hands laced behind his head, as relaxed and happy as I'd ever seen him. He grinned at me like he was the king of the world. "Peep, look how far we've come from living on a dollar a day."

I sighed with satisfaction and nestled into his shoulder. I knew it filled Steve up to know he could afford a blow-out party like this. He had a right to be proud, and I was certainly proud of him. It felt great to give our friends and loved ones a vacation in Reno, and of course Steve loved playing the host—he was always at the heart of the action, and wherever we went, people wanted to be close to him.

But the truth was, I'd been happy back when it was just the two of us and we were scraping by on a dollar a day. I loved that summer when Steve lay on the deck and told me my row was crooked while I planted seeds in the garden. Now he was almost always surrounded by people who wanted a piece of his attention, and too often I had the uncomfortable feeling that I had to stand in line along with everyone else. These moments when I had Steve all to myself were precious to me.

On our last night in Reno I won five thousand dollars on a five-dollar slot machine. Steve didn't see me rake in the loot, because he was busy at the black jack table. I tiptoed into the elevator with the cash, rode up to our motel room and sprinkled hundred dollar bills from the door to our bed, then put on my prettiest peignoir and posed with money scattered all around me on the bedspread.

When Steve walked in, his eyes followed the path of money trailing from the door to our bed. He looked at me and lifted his palms, as if to say "What's going on?"

I giggled, opened my arms wide and wiggled my fingers. "I won!"

There it was: his trademark grin. A flash of white teeth, a lazy, cocky glance that slowly embraced every inch of me, and a wicked twinkle in his eyes. Whenever he smiled at me like that, I melted.

Our next big event was Stephanie's wedding to Scott. Steve really liked Scott, and when Scott formally asked him for permission to marry Stephanie, Steve was impressed. For the next few months Steph and I spent hours on the phone as we went over every detail of the plans, the guest list, the menu and the costs. By now this girl and I were so close it felt like she was my own daughter, and when she told me she wanted a real church wedding with all the trimmings, I did everything I could to help her make her dream come true.

On the day of the wedding, Steph shimmered with pre-wedding jitters, and the tension radiated from her in waves you could feel from twenty feet away. It probably would have done her good to run around the block before the ceremony—she was pretty keyed-up and snapped at Dorothy a few times—but I seemed to be her rock, her calming sedative.

Once the wedding march began, Stephanie looked like a princess in a fairy tale as Steve walked her down the aisle. He told me later it was the proudest moment of his life.

Dorothy was great. We'd been co-parents for so long we felt like a team, and she'd always been one of my dearest friends since the day Steve called her to come over and pluck my eyebrows. Dorothy was supposed to be escorted down the aisle before me, but she took me by the arm and said, "We're walking down the aisle together."

And so we did. The groomsman held out his arms to both

of us, and the three of us walked down the aisle together, with Dorothy on one arm and me on the other.

In early 1994 Steve and I both fell in love with twelve acres of open land that came up for sale on Newark Road. It was surrounded by forty acres of woods in a gorgeous rural setting outside Lapeer. We bought the parcel, and a few months later we found a house blueprint we both liked in a magazine. In June 1994, we hired a company to dig the basement.

Steve bought a bulldozer, nicknamed it Baby and it quickly became his favorite toy. He was like a little kid in a candy factory with that bulldozer. He loved running it, and he spent hours on the bulldozer to put in the driveway and move dirt for the walkout basement. He did all the groundwork for the yard. He bought a used backhoe, moved tons of rocks and dug some small ponds in the back yard. Later, he envisioned a waterfall going into one of these ponds, and he commissioned our tree man to design and construct it.

For six months we worked our tails off on the new house. Steve installed all the oak beams. Larry helped him put in the kitchen, while Larry's wife Chris helped me stain and varnish all the woodwork. Steve and Stevie did most of the painting. We worked on the house every night after working all day at the plant, and drove home to Bridgeman Trail in a daze at nine or ten. We barely had enough energy to brush our teeth before we collapsed in bed.

I wanted to be in our new house by Christmas, so we moved on December 23, in the middle of a snowstorm. That night I stayed in the Bridgeman Trail house to give it one last thorough cleaning. As I scrubbed the counters in the kitchen I thought of all the cookies, breads, cakes and pies I'd baked over the years, all the pickles and preserves I'd canned in this little old kitchen that I loved. By the time I got out the vacuum to go over the carpet, I was crying so hard the tears were dripping off my chin.

This had been our first real home together. *Why are we doing this?* I asked myself. *We've been so happy here! Why do we have to move?*

Both of us loved the old house. This was where we'd built our prototype for the fan, and lived on the produce from the garden while we waited for our business to grow. After we'd rented the house for five years, the owner had finally sold it to us in 1986. Our dogs were buried in a memorial plot in the back yard. I'd refinished all the cabinets by myself. Steve and Larry had built a beautiful deck out back, and we'd both toiled over the landscaping. It seemed insane to leave after we'd had so many good times here, and worked so hard to make it a home. It felt like tearing off a limb to let go, and the more I cleaned every nook and cranny of each room, the more miserable I felt.

That evening Steve came over to help me finish up. We worked in silence, and I knew he was having second thoughts too. I traced the countertop with my fingers, reluctant to stop scrubbing, but I'd already polished it to a high gloss and if I kept rubbing it I'd probably scratch the finish. Finally I turned to Steve, who was sweeping a few invisible crumbs off the floor with the same lack of enthusiasm.

"I don't want to leave." My throat closed, and tears filled my eyes.

He put his arms around my waist and squeezed me tight.

We stared at the empty living room, and bare walls stared back at us. All our furniture and belongings were at the new house. The Bridgeman Trail house looked like an orphan now, as if our existence over the last thirteen years had been erased.

"We must be crazy," I whispered.

"I know," he said unhappily. "I know."

The next morning I woke up in my new bed in my new house, dragged myself away from the warmth of Steve's body next to mine, went downstairs and looked around. The new place was a mess. Boxes were everywhere, piled haphazardly in the wrong rooms, with boxes of dishes in the bedrooms and boxes of linens in the kitchen and boxes of clothes in the basement. *Merry Christmas,* I thought bitterly, and went back upstairs, crawled in bed with Steve and cried against his shoulder while he held me.

Neither one of us liked the new house. Our old house on Bridgman Trail had already been sold, or we would have moved back. The new house was just too big. We couldn't hear each other, and had to shout between rooms. Every night during our Christmas vacation we talked about selling it so we could find something smaller, but we were both exhausted from the move and couldn't face the thought of dislocating our lives once more.

A few weeks later, I woke up one morning and stumbled downstairs to make coffee in my brand-new kitchen. I had to admit, the kitchen windows that overlooked the yard were beautifully framed, and the morning sun cast glowing squares of light across the octagonal kitchen table we'd placed in the breakfast nook.

As I yawned and gazed out the kitchen window, I saw a dark shape materialize at the edge of the woods in the back yard. I squinted to get a better look, and saw a smaller shape emerge from the shadowed trees.

Deer! My heart skittered with rising excitement as I watched a doe and her fawn ease out into the open field. Another dark silhouette appeared, and another.

"Steve!" I yelled up the stairs. "Come down here! You've got to see this!"

By the time he came downstairs and walked over to join me, there were more than twenty deer grazing in our back yard. He stared out the window, shot me a grin and sat down at the kitchen table to watch the deer nibble at the frozen, broken stubble in the field.

That was the beginning of our love affair with the new house. Eventually we put corn and salt blocks out for the deer, and within a few months it wasn't unusual to look out in the morning and see sixty or seventy deer grazing in the fields surrounding us.

In December 1996, Steve went to the Louisville show and came back with the mother of all headaches. He told me his head hurt so much it felt like it would blow up. He'd taken Advil, Tylenol, and pressed bags of frozen peas to his head, but nothing could touch that headache. He begged me to press my hands against both sides of his head and apply all the pressure I could. It didn't help.

Finally I convinced him to go to the doctor.

We sat together in the exam room while the doctor checked Steve's blood pressure. As the doctor released the air pressure from the cuff, he let out a low whistle. "Two-twenty over one-ten. You'd better go to the hospital and have an echocardiogram on your heart."

"Now?" I asked.

"*Now.*"

We barely said a word in the car on the way to the hospital. I was sick with worry, unsure what was wrong, and Steve continued to hold his head with both hands, obviously crippled by the pain.

We had the echocardiogram done, and the EKG doctor insisted that Steve check into the hospital immediately for further tests.

By the time we arrived at the admissions desk my insides were shaking, I was so scared. Steve was pale, beads of sweat had popped across his forehead, and from time to time his hands trembled as if he had Parkinson's disease. A team of nurses and orderlies put him on a gurney and wheeled him off to another room. I desperately wanted to go with him to find out what was happening, but they wouldn't let me go until I finished filling out the stack of forms.

At last they led me to Steve's room, where I saw him stretched out on a hospital bed, surrounded by nurses who were busy hooking him up to heart monitors, blood pressure cuffs and an IV line. The machines beeped with ominous, erratic sounds. The heart monitor above his bed flashed numbers that changed every split second. By now Steve was sweating profusely from the pain, and as soon as he saw me he begged me to go get help, to find someone who would give him a shot or a pill or anything for his headache.

The nurses told Steve they couldn't give him anything for the pain until the doctor ordered it, and no one knew where the doctor was. Panic flooded through me as I rushed back and forth from Steve's bed to the front desk and back to Steve with the bad news that no one knew where the doctor was or how long it would take him to get there.

We waited. It was hell for Steve, and hell for me as I watched him writhe in bed with his hands pressed to his head.

Two hours later the doctor finally breezed through the door, put on his stethoscope and listened to Steve's heart and lungs. He lifted the chart from the foot of the hospital bed and leafed through it, oblivious to Steve's labored breathing.

By now Steve was almost in tears from the pain, and I could hear the strain in his voice as he begged for relief. "You've got to give me something. My head's about to explode."

The doctor murmured a noncommittal "Hmm" as he continued to read the chart.

"What's going on?" I asked his doctor. "What's the matter with him?"

"Heart failure," the doctor replied matter-of-factly.

All the air went out of me, as if I'd been sucker punched by those two little words: *Heart failure.*

I opened my mouth but it took a few seconds before I could get the words out. "Will he be all right?"

The doctor shrugged. "He has a lot of fluid built up around his heart."

"What can you do for him?"

"Right now? He has an IV for blood pressure medication going, so the headache should ease up in a few hours."

"I can't wait that long," Steve gasped.

The doctor nodded, held up one finger and walked out. A few minutes later he reappeared with a nurse, who carried a hypodermic. He told Steve to roll over to one side. The nurse swabbed a patch of skin on Steve's rump with alcohol and gave him the injection.

"What is it?" I asked the doctor.

"Demerol."

Within a minute, the lines disappeared from Steve's face, and he relaxed back against the pillow, his eyes half closed. He looked drunk, but he was still awake. I could feel every cell in my body open and release, almost as if I'd received the injection myself.

The doctor went on talking as casually as if he'd just swatted a mosquito. "Eventually you'll need a heart catheter so we can see if there's any serious blockage of the arteries."

"What's a heart catheter?" I asked.

"It's a simple procedure to examine blood flow to the heart."

"How simple?" Steve mumbled.

"We insert a thin plastic tube into a coronary artery and introduce a dye to test the pumping ability of the heart muscle."

Steve shook his head. His voice was slurred from the drug, but he sounded stubborn as ever. "I'll think about it, but I'm not crazy about having dye put in me."

"Come on, Stephen," I pleaded with him. "You need the test."

He refused to meet my gaze. "My dad had a stroke when they put that dye into him."

"You're not going to die," I told him. *There's no way I'm going to become a widow at forty-one, buddy!* "I won't let you die. But you have to get this done, or you will."

"Give it a rest," he muttered. "There's nothing wrong with my heart."

The doctor checked his watch. "I'll pop in later." And then he floated out the door.

For the next six days, I spent hours staring at that heart monitor over Steve's bed. I drove the nurses crazy, asking questions until I understood every single number that flashed on the screen, and I grilled them on all the medicines in the IV bags until I became deeply familiar with the difference between the nitroglycerine, diuretics and blood pressure medicine. The diuretics removed excess fluid from around his heart. Nitro opened his veins for better blood flow. The blood pressure medicine was supposed to bring his circulatory system under control.

The good news was that it all seemed to be working.

After a week in the hospital, the fluid around Steve's heart began to subside, and he told me he was feeling better.

But when he came home, he collapsed.

"Your husband has three arteries that are totally blocked. Unfortunately they're too small to insert a stent—he's going to need open-heart surgery."

Steve and I sat in the doctor's office. As soon as I heard the doctor give us the diagnosis, I felt my body go numb. I couldn't absorb it. It felt as if there was a barrier of frosted glass between me and the man in the white coat who sat in front of me with a cool, matter-of-fact expression on his face.

Steve stared out the window at the gray squares of December light and waved a hand. "Let the games begin."

By now Steve had developed a fatalistic attitude toward his heart that made me more and more panicked. *What if you die?* I thought. *What on earth will I do then?*

"Until he has the surgery, it's imperative that he avoid all unnecessary excitement." The doctor gave me a hard look. "No smoking. No drinking. No exertion. Keep him as calm and relaxed as you can." He scribbled out a prescription for nitroglycerine, tore it off the pad and held it out to me.

I nodded. I had to tell myself to stop nodding. I had to tell myself to unclench the fingers of my right hand from the wrist of my left hand and take the prescription. I had to tell myself to stand up and leave the office. My heart skipped and jerked like a fish out of water, and I could not take a deep breath.

For the next few days, I kept busy. I pestered everyone I knew for advice, recommendations, information. But I moved within a cold fog, a slow-motion gap between me and reality. Fear seized me every morning, the second I woke up, as soon as I thought about the surgery. But what choice did we have? Steve was only fifty-six. *Too young to die.*

We put his name down on the waiting list for surgery at Cleveland Clinic, and awaited a call with our appointment date.

Two weeks later, on January 4, 1997, the phone rang in the middle of the night.

Steve grunted, rolled over and fumbled for the receiver on the bedside table. "Hello?"

After a brief silence, I felt him sit up. "Yes. Okay. How—? Okay. Be right there."

He threw back the covers and bolted out of bed. "Peep, the plant's on fire. Get up! We have to go, now!"

Electrified by his words, I leaped out of bed, pulled on a pair of jeans and a sweatshirt and struggled to put on my sneakers. He ran down the stairs and out into the night, and I followed close behind. It was eighteen degrees, with a strong wind out of the southwest that sucked the warmth from my body. Immediately I knew we needed more clothes, but we were flooded with adrenaline and there was no question of going back. We jumped in the car and sped toward the plant, while snow blew in horizontal streams against the windshield.

"How bad is it?" I asked.

"I don't know."

"Maybe it's not too bad."

Steve gunned the engine, and we streaked past the Imlay City exit. When we were eight or ten miles away from the plant, we could see an orange glow in the northeast sky. As we drove closer, the glow became brighter.

"Holy shit," I whispered.

Steve peered through the streaming snow that coated the windshield between each slap of the wipers. "The whole place must be on fire."

We knew by the glow that this was no small blaze. When we finally pulled up to the plant, we saw fire trucks, firemen and hoses spread over a quarter mile. Sirens wailed in the black night, and cruiser lights sent red and blue strobes against the pillars of black smoke that rose from the building and joined the dark mass of storm clouds above us.

Steve and I bolted from the car to find the nearest fireman. Four inches of fresh snow had turned the parking lot into a lake of slush, and as soon as my sneakers hit the ground, my feet were soaked. The wind cut through my sweatshirt like a knife.

Steve grabbed the fireman by his elbow and shouted over the noise. "We're the owners! What happened? How'd it start?"

In the glare of the firelight I could see the fireman's face was black with soot, his eyes eerily white around the irises. He had to yell over the wind and the crackle of flames. "The fire above the ceiling—spread east and west and then dropped like a fifteen thousand square foot fireball."

Steve and I gave each other an anguished look. This meant the entire production area, wood shop, oak storage area and the plastic and wire stocking area had already burst into flames.

"What about the offices?" Steve shouted.

"We don't have a key," the fireman yelled. "We've got our hands full with the fire on the main floor."

"We have to go in," Steve said.

The fireman shook his head. "The fire's too big. We got six different departments here and we still don't have it licked. Used up all the water in the Capac tower. We'll have to truck in more."

Steve wiped his face with both hands, and I saw his fingers begin to tremble. How could we watch our dream go up in smoke and not do anything? Flames licked the sky with bright orange tongues while columns of smoke billowed from the windows.

Snow whipped against my face, and the blizzard swirled around us.

Suddenly Steve ran to the office door, and I scurried after him.

"Hey!" the fireman shouted. "You can't go in there! The smoke could kill you!"

I struggled to unlock the door while Steve fumbled in his coat pocket and tipped a nitroglycerine tablet under his tongue. Most people have pain in their chest or down their arm during a heart attack, but I knew Steve's pain was in his jaw. When I saw him hold his jaw with a look of misery on his face, my panic ratcheted higher.

Keep him calm, the doctor had said. *No excitement. No stress.*

The fireman pursued us to the door, and when I finally wrenched the door open, he extended his arm to bar our entry. "Hold it."

"Just give us a minute to get our files," Steve pleaded.

The fireman peered inside, then nodded. "Make it fast, and I mean *damn* fast."

Steve pushed through the doorway, and I plunged after him. Immediately, the heat sucked the air out of my lungs. Smoke filled the offices with a poisonous fog, but the flames hadn't reached our files yet.

"I'll do this!" I yelled at him. "You wait here!"

Steve ignored me and made a beeline for his office. *God damn it,* I thought.

I raced into my office and grabbed the hard drive for the computer, the ledger cards of accounts and the file of orders that needed to be shipped. Everything was black with soot.

When we headed back to the parking lot, Steve never even looked at me. He moved so slowly, and several times he had to bend over to catch his breath. I was terrified he was having a heart attack.

"Will you please wait outside?" I shouted.

He shook his head and went back into the hot, smoke-filled darkness of the building.

Please let him be okay, I whispered. *Please let him be okay.*

I ran to my office and gathered an armload of files. When we finally emerged into the cold air of the parking lot, I coughed and hacked up black phlegm and shivered violently in the cold air. My sneakers were wet. My feet were freezing. My breath came in ragged, painful gasps, but I knew I had to go back in there.

Steve hunched over suddenly, as if he'd been kicked in the chest.

The sight of him bent over like that pierced me to the core. *No, no, no!* The thought rose up in me so loud it felt like a scream.

He trembled all over as though he were being electrocuted, and I watched him fumble in his coat pocket for the vial of pills. His hand shook as he lifted the bottle to his mouth. He was white as a ghost. His color had been bad for a couple of months but now he was paler than I'd ever seen him. The doctor had warned him that the circulation in his legs was terrible, and the cold only made it worse.

I took him by the shoulders. "*Wait.* Let me do this.*"

Steve shook me off and hobbled back inside.

I ran back to my office, stacked our official Patent and the Fleetwood vendor award on top of my typewriter and staggered back out. Steve emerged from the building and crossed the parking lot. He was limping and shaking uncontrollably, and I knew it wasn't just from the cold. He waved to his brother Larry, who had just pulled up. Other employees, friends and family streamed into the parking lot. Someone pulled Steve into one of the cars to get warm, and when I walked over, Larry opened his truck for me and left me there. My feet were wet, frozen, and I couldn't stop shaking. The smell of smoke clung to my hair, clothes and skin, and when I looked in the rear view mirror my face was covered in soot.

I began to cry. My face ached from the cold. My throat stung from smoke, and rasping sobs shook my whole body. I wanted my husband. I wanted Steve. I just wanted to hold him and be held by him. I wanted to talk to him about what had happened, and I wasn't even sure which car he was in, and besides, I was too damn cold to move. I wept bitter, angry tears. *Why had this happened? Where was Steve? Why wasn't he trying to find me? And oh sweet baby Jesus, what if Steve is having a heart attack right now?*

Misery sat on my chest like an anvil I couldn't lift.

Larry opened the truck door and touched my knee. "You okay?"

"I'm so cold," I sobbed.

"Can I get you anything?"

"Boots," I said. "My feet are soaked."

"Take off your wet sneakers and socks and let the heater blow on them." He cranked the heater fan.

"Is Steve okay?" I was afraid to ask, but I had to know.

"He's in shock. Shaking pretty bad."

I nodded, unable to speak.

Larry gazed at the burning building, then turned to me with a desolate look on his face. "I'll be back, okay? You sit tight."

I sat in Larry's truck and watched our business burn. No amount of insurance could repay us for the love and attention we'd lavished on this centerpiece of our lives. We had just had the floors refinished over the Christmas break. The addition was only two years old, and now it was gone. Everything we had worked so hard for twelve and a half years to achieve was all going up in smoke. Mesmerized by the destruction, I watched the fire until there was nothing left but charred timbers, twisted metal and ash.

People came and went. Someone brought me boots and a coat. Daylight turned the blackness into a thin gray mist, and smoke hung over the parking lot like a stinking shroud. I staggered from one smoldering pile to another, searching for anything I could rescue. Steve moved in a tight throng of employees, relatives, friends, customers and people who had stopped to see the fire. They swallowed him into different cars and trucks, and he passed from one vehicle to another. Wherever he went, he was pursued by knots of people who immersed him in gabbling, excited conversation.

It was late afternoon before Steve and I staggered back home, and a flood of relatives and employees followed us inside. The phone kept ringing. Over and over again we had to repeat the horrifying facts for friends who had just heard the news: our whole business was gone, burned to heaps of smoking rubble.

In the past two days, Steve and I had slept only two hours. He was still limping, shaking, holding his jaw in pain. People trampled through our living room to grab him and beg for reassurance. They were all worried they might not have jobs anymore. It was bedlam, and Steve did nothing to encourage anyone to leave.

By then I was desperate to be alone with Steve. Couldn't he see we needed to grieve and comfort each other and talk about what had happened? I was furious at Steve for taking chances with his health. I was angry that he sat in a car with other people in that godforsaken parking lot and never tried to find me, so we could face the catastrophe together. Everyone kept crowding around him looking for answers we didn't have, and he did nothing to stop them. His focus was still on the fire. He had never once asked me how I felt.

I felt guilty for having these thoughts. I knew I was being selfish. These people tracking soot through my living room were just as scared as I was. But at that moment, if anyone offered me the choice to go back to our little life of living on a dollar a day, I would have given up everything—our business, our big new house, our savings, everything!—just to have Steve to myself again.

Finally Steve and I escaped the crowd in the living room and went up to our bedroom to take a shower. We were both filthy. My clothes reeked of smoke, my skin was coated with soot and every time I licked my lips I tasted ash. As soon as we were in the master bath, he locked the door behind us. At long last, we were alone together.

He turned the shower on, left the water running and then looked at me—really *looked* at me—for the first time all day. Now that we were alone, he could be himself. He didn't have to be this bigger-than-life character, the godfather who had all the answers, the one who took care of everybody. It was just the two of us.

For a moment we stood there and stared at each other, and I used my thumb to wipe the soot from his cheek.

As soon as I touched him, his face crumpled. He reached for me, wrapped his arms around me and wept.

Please don't die, I thought. *Please, please don't leave me. That is the one thing I can't handle right now.*

I held him the way I held our kids when they were little. I stroked his back and steadied my breathing to force him to breathe more slowly. His breath came in gulps as he sobbed. I just held him and let him cry. Neither of us said a word.

This is what I had longed for and waited for all day. Just the two of us, alone, a husband and wife, not business owners with a house full of employees who were terrified they wouldn't have a job. Finally we were here by ourselves, without anyone looking at us or firing questions at us that we couldn't answer.

At long last he took a deep, shuddering breath and pulled away, his hands still on my shoulders. He licked his finger, stroked a smudge of ash from my face and smiled. His breathing had finally eased, and he was able to stand up straight.

"Jesus, we've got a shit-load of work ahead. Couldn't be a worse time for open-heart surgery."

I held my gaze steady on his face. "Oh no you don't, buddy. You are not postponing this surgery."

He laughed. For the first time all day his face looked relaxed, open. "You okay?"

I'm fine."

We both knew it was a lie, but I gave him my best smile. We

stepped out of our clothes, opened the glass door of the shower, and entered the stream of warm water.

❧ Chapter Thirteen ❧

Our work to rebuild the business started immediately. Jack heard about a building we might be able to rent in Imlay City, and after we had a quick lunch we drove out there to look at the place. We rented it that same day, while the ashes of our old building were still smoldering.

The girls who worked in our office came to our house and we called our customers to let them know about the fire and assure them their orders would be filled and delivered as soon as possible. Larry called the vendors to get raw inventory and the equipment we needed, and Jim, our tooling man built new jigs and a screen melt machine.

Steve was still shaky. I was terrified he would have a heart attack. He was so pale. He couldn't walk a hundred yards without breaking into a sweat, so the rest of us ran circles around him while he broadcast advice, directions and encouragement. He wanted to help with the physical work, but we wouldn't let him.

Steve's sister Susie helped me set up files in the new office, and we plundered the local office supply stores to buy everything we needed, from computers to pens and pencils. We met with our computer man to drop off the hard drive we'd salvaged from the fire and see what he could recover. Tonya and I estimated how much office equipment would fit into a thousand square foot office space and ordered furniture to fit. There would be eight of us jammed in that thousand square foot office, a big change from our spacious ten thousand square foot office in the burned building in Capac. Our old plant had been thirty-two thousand square feet. Now we had to set up a new plant in eight thousand square feet.

Our employees continued to burn the midnight oil to help us. There were many twenty hour days when Steve and I lived on three or four hours of sleep at night. Larry pushed himself to the brink of exhaustion as he tried to take the load off Steve, and spent hours on the phone to find numbers for suppliers and order enough inventory to start manufacturing again. Buck raced back and forth in our forklift truck to unload raw materials from the semis that poured through our lot. Jack practically lived at the plant while he and Steve planned the layout of the production area.

Steve and I had no time to talk or even react to all the changes that swirled around us. We were both so focused on rebuilding every single part of the business that we barely had time to think, and we moved from one emergency to another. Life was a blur.

One Friday afternoon, Steve and I were hard at work at our desks. Paperwork from the insurance company covered my blotter, and I felt overwhelmed by the data they'd just requested: an estimate of the daily loss of income, expenses incurred after the fire, and a million other details I didn't want to think about. But this was my life now. My head was immersed in figures that reflected our loss.

Suddenly I heard Steve stifle a gasp.

I looked up, my senses on full alert. "What's the matter?"

"I don't feel so good," he admitted. His face was almost white. A film of sweat popped out on his forehead, and his hand trembled as he wiped away the dampness on his face.

I jumped up and crossed the room. "Lie down!"

There was nowhere to lie down but the hard office floor, but he didn't argue. He raised himself slowly out of his chair and crumpled to the thinly carpeted concrete. I helped him stretch out his legs until he was lying completely flat.

In a panic, I scrambled through my lunch box and found a small plastic bottle of orange juice. I knelt on the floor, cradled his head in my lap and lifted the juice to his lips. His hand shook as he touched the bottle and took a few sips. He shivered and stared up at me with fear in his eyes.

Our eyes locked and his fear poured into me. He couldn't control what was happening inside his body. My own heart slammed against my ribs.

"Should I call 911?" I asked.

"No," he muttered. "Just give me a second here."

I picked up his hand and kissed the inside of his wrist. His pulse bucked and jerked under my lips.

If he dies … I couldn't even complete that thought. It was unthinkable.

I tried to steady my breathing. I tried to pretend it was the most natural thing in the world to sit here on the floor of our office with Steve stretched out flat with his head in my lap.

Everything will be all right. I repeated the phrase in my head as I pressed his hand to my face and willed his heart to find its rhythm again. *Everything will be all right.* It had to be. I smoothed the hair away from his forehead, found a calm voice to speak in and used it. "Hang on, buddy. You'll be fine."

He nodded, and after a minute or two his breath came easier. "Let me up," he said. "I've got to make sure these orders get done."

On January 15, 1997, just eleven days after the fire, we were back in business. Production was limited, of course. We needed a rivet machine, and it hadn't come in yet, so we had to rivet the hinges onto every dome by hand, which made it a much slower process. But we built five hundred fans that day.

We loaded our biggest delivery truck with the orders that were the highest priority. We could have put them on UPS, but they wouldn't have been delivered until the next afternoon in Indiana. There were customers who needed their fans first thing the next morning, and we were determined to fill those orders and deliver them on time. Steve's brother Buck drove the loaded truck to his house in Lansing after work, then rose at three in the morning to make deliveries to Newmar, Holiday Rambler, Fleetwood, Travel Supreme, and Sunnybrook.

A major snowstorm hit Indiana that day, and most of those plants were closed. Buck and Larry heated up the phone lines to find workers who could take the shipments, and by the end of the day every single fan had been safely delivered.

"We did it." I grinned at Steve, and he sat back in his chair and grinned back at me.

"Piece of cake." He put his feet up on his desk.

I looked around the office and out to the production line, where our employees were still working to get the business back on its feet. Every one of them had given up time with their kids, time with their wives, time with their husbands, and they'd been running on so little sleep they looked like zombies. It overwhelmed me for a moment, how much everyone had given to us. They'd worked until they were ready to drop. The fatigue I felt was no more than what any one of them felt, and I was so tired I could barely talk.

Only one hurdle lay between us and the happily-ever-after. Steve and I didn't talk about it, but we knew it was getting closer every day, and I lay in bed at night in a state of dread. In two weeks we'd drive to Cleveland and check Steve into the hospital for his heart surgery. I was terrified of the operation that lay ahead.

Steve had his surgery on February 6, 1997.

By the time we arrived at the hospital, I was sick to my stomach with anxiety. The hallways looked like an assembly line, with people on gurneys waiting for their turn at surgery. Steve and I followed a nurse to a cubicle where he undressed, and I helped him put on his hospital gown.

"You're going to be just fine," I told him.

He let out a bitter laugh. "You know I'm not going to live past sixty-five. None of the men in my family lived to see seventy."

This wasn't the first time he told me he'd die young. But now his words stabbed me, and I was instantly furious. "Stop it! If you're convinced you'll die, you will. You'll talk your body into it. "

What will I do if he dies? I had no friends of my own. My whole life was devoted to living with him, working with him and waiting on him hand and foot. I'd made him the center of my life. I yanked the strings on the back of his gown and almost ripped the material as I tightened the knots.

The doctor breezed into the room. "This will take a couple of hours," he told me. "Try to be patient. There won't be any updates during the surgery, but I'm sure everything will go smoothly and we'll have some good news for you soon."

I nodded. My jaw felt tight as a vise. "Okay."

Steve tried to smile as they wheeled him away, and gave me a thumbs-up salute. I lifted both hands to show him my fingers were crossed.

One hour went by. *I can do this*, I told myself. *Drink coffee from the vending machine. Pretend to read this magazine. Turn the page. Turn another page. Check the clock on the wall. Maybe the clock is broken? No, the second hand is moving. Have another cup of coffee. Walk around the waiting room six times. Twelve times. Twenty-four times. If I do thirty more laps of the waiting room, there will be news, everything will be all right, Steve will be ready to see me and he'll wink and smile and the world will feel whole and safe again.*

Two hours later, I was a basket case. I pestered every nurse, orderly and doctor I saw with questions. "They said it wouldn't take more than two hours! What happened? Is Steve all right? When will they be done? Is there any news at all?"

"No," they said. "Didn't the surgeon tell you? There won't be any updates until the surgery is over."

After three hours in the waiting room, I was paralyzed with fear. There was no news. The clock was my enemy. I sat on the edge of the waiting room couch and prayed. *Please, please, please, please, please. Please don't let him die.*

After four hours, I was in despair. My cuticles were bleeding. I'd had so many cups of coffee my hands trembled with caffeine jitters, and I couldn't take a deep breath. After four hours on an operating table … it couldn't be good news. Not after four hours. Steve was dying, or he was already dead.

After five hours, my mind disconnected from the rest of my body and my awareness floated off to a distant corner of the ceiling, while my body remained glued to its chair. My legs were numb. My hands were freezing cold. I was thirsty and I had to pee, but none of that mattered any more. If my vigil in the waiting room kept Steve alive, I would wait forever.

Steve was in surgery for six hours.

When I finally saw the surgeon come out into the waiting room, I rose from the chair and tottered toward him.

"Come this way." He walked briskly down the hallway to his office while I trailed behind him.

Would he lead me to his office if he had good news? Was this standard procedure, or did he only do this when the patient died?

My legs seemed far away, while my head felt light as a helium balloon.

The doctor held the door open for me, gestured to a chair, walked behind his desk and fell into his seat with a sigh. He cleared his throat. "The surgery was a little more complicated than we thought it would be."

Don't tell me this, I thought.

"The damage was more extensive than we realized. Your husband had five arteries that were blocked. Two arteries found a different route for the blood, so we left those in place. We took two mammary arteries and an artery from his leg to bypass the other three blocked arteries."

I watched the surgeon's mouth move and I heard the words come out, but they seemed to camouflage a deeper meaning I couldn't grasp. "So he's all right?"

He lifted a shoulder. "He has an aortic aneurysm that we'll have to continue to monitor, but otherwise the surgery went quite well."

Aneurysm. I struggled to remember what the word meant.

He held his thumb and forefinger an inch apart. "An aneurysm is a bulge in the aorta, like a bulge on an over-inflated inner tube. It's fairly small now, but if it gets bigger…" He stretched his fingers wide in a starburst, then let his hand fall back in his lap.

I stared at his hand.

The look on my face must have alarmed him, because he leaned forward and spoke quickly in an exaggerated, cheery tone. "We can fix the aneurysm when it gets bigger. Just make sure he takes it easy until then. It's important that he remain relaxed and calm."

"Can I see him?"

"Of course. But he's very weak, and still unconscious from the anesthetic. You'll have to limit your visit to no more than five minutes."

"Five minutes," I agreed. I stood up.

The doctor led me out of the office, down the corridor, past the swinging doors of the intensive care unit. He opened the door to a room at the end of the hall.

I walked in, and the sight of Steve in his hospital bed hit me like a kick in the chest. His eyes were closed, and his face was so bloated he was almost unrecognizable. He was not asleep. This was different from sleep. It was the place between sleep and death. A mask covered his mouth, and a ventilator by his bed made ominous whooshing sounds as it puffed air into his lungs. An IV tapped a vein in his neck. There were tubes coming out of both sides of his stomach.

He looked like he was eighty years old. He looked like a stranger.

My knees buckled and I swayed, reeled back and bumped into the doctor. He grabbed my arm and lowered me to a chair, then asked the nurse to bring a wet washcloth to put on my face.

I squeezed my eyes shut, silently screamed at myself to *get a grip,* then took a deep breath. Steve had just been cracked open and poked and prodded for the past six hours. No wonder he looked beat up. I brushed away the washcloth the nurse offered, rose to my feet and crossed to his bedside.

I kissed his forehead and whispered in his ear. "Hey, buddy. Looks like you made it."

It was eerie, to stroke his slack face. There was no response. No flutter of his eyelids, no smile, no movement at all. He was so loud in real life, but now his silence chilled me.

When Steve finally emerged from the hospital, he had a twelve-inch scar of deep purple welts on his sternum.

"Look at that Zipper," he said proudly when he unbuttoned his shirt. "Now I know how Humpty-Dumpty felt. All I lacked was a toe tag."

They'd cut an artery from his leg and two arteries from his

chest and sewn them to his heart. They'd pumped him full of drugs and messed around with his insides for six hours. But within a few weeks, it was clear that he had more energy. The circulation in his legs improved, so it was less painful for him to walk around the house, and his color was much better.

Of course there were limitations. It took him a month before he could climb a set of stairs. He couldn't walk farther than a hundred yards, he couldn't lift anything heavier than a coffee cup, and we were both aware of the ticking time-bomb in his chest.

With the specter of the aneurysm hanging over us, we couldn't relax. How could we plunge back into the passionate life we'd enjoyed as a couple, when orgasm might mean sudden death? We were afraid to have sex. The blood pressure medication diminished Steve's desire, and as the days and weeks and months passed without any sign from him that he thought about sex or wanted sex, I realized this part of our lives together was over. Our nighttime ritual included a long, tight hug before we turned over and went to sleep. But that was all.

Privately, I grieved the loss. Sex with Steve had always brought out the most reckless, playful part of me. Once when I picked him up at the airport after a business trip, I wore a coat with nothing on underneath it. I flashed him while we were still in the terminal, and he groaned out loud and pulled me to him as we walked out to the parking lot. I tore myself away and ran ahead of him, laughing, and flirted up the hem of the coat so he could see my bare rump. By the time we got into the car, we were so aroused we were both ready to explode.

I was only forty years old. I missed sex, and I especially

missed the afterglow of sex, when we gasped and laughed and flopped back in a tangle of limbs, relaxed and happy and fulfilled. Sex purged the anxiety from our day. No matter what trouble was brewing with the business or the kids or our employees, sex could erase all of it.

Eventually we developed a domestic routine that brought small, unexpected pleasures, and a new kind of intimacy. Steve became an avid crossword puzzle fan, and worked one or two crosswords every day with my help. We went to the plant most Saturdays to check the fax machine for orders, and afterwards we went out to breakfast. I waxed my feet on Sundays to moisturize them, and I began waxing Steve's feet too.

"Did you ever think you'd let your wife wax your feet?" I teased him.

"Never," he said, and turned a page of the newspaper. "But now I can't get enough of it."

Of course we wrangled endlessly about what constituted a heart-healthy menu. We went back and forth in an endless debate over his doctor's recommended diet and what Steve thought was healthy. His favorite meal was still the All-American Dinner, and he wasn't about to stop eating fried food. He had total faith in his cholesterol medication.

"Put that down!" I yelped when I caught him eating French fries.

He popped another French fry into his mouth. "I've got my Pac-Man pills. They gobble up all the bad stuff."

I had to admit, Steve looked healthier than he had in a long time, and every day he seemed more and more like his old self. Funny. Ambitious as ever. Cracking jokes, making big plans about the landscaping projects he wanted to accomplish that summer. He gave up drinking, which was a nice change of pace—now he was *my* designated driver!

But the fire, the push to re-establish the business in a new space, the fear and pain of his heart surgery—and the fear of the surgery to come, if the aneurysm grew larger—it all took a toll on us. Every time he had the slightest physical twinge I was scared, and whenever he put his hand on his chest, my senses went on full alert.

"Are you having heart pain?"

"I'm fine. It's just comfortable to put my hand here."

"You're not lying to me, are you?"

He laughed and shook his head. We had this dialogue a hundred times. I knew he didn't always tell me when he had chest pain, and I kept a keen eye on him whenever we were in the same room together, which was nearly all the time. It was exhausting.

We have to get away, I thought. *Somewhere warm, safe, easy. Somewhere we can heal.*

I knew exactly where to go.

Ten thousand feet below us the coastline of Florida curved into the wide bay of Charlotte Harbor. We were nearly there. Another hour and we'd kick back in our suite at the Diamond Head Beach Resort in Fort Myers. It was our guaranteed-good-time getaway, and when we visited the hotel the year before, we'd had a blast.

Our friends Perry and Faye glanced across the aisle at us and grinned like school kids who had skipped class to go to the beach. The beach! Sun! Warmth! Seven whole days away from the business! I could hardly believe it. It felt like a dream, and as far as I was concerned, I was off duty as of *right now!* The weight of the past four months fell away, and I reveled in my good fortune. We were both free of the worries at the plant that had dogged us all year.

When the stewardess came by to see if we wanted drinks, Steve slipped a hundred dollar bill into her hand and whispered "This is just for grins." It worked. She glowed at him, and she was still lit up when she came back with our order. I smiled to myself and knocked back a gulp of vodka. If Steve felt good enough to tip the stewardess a hundred dollars, he was feeling better, and that meant I was safe.

Steve nudged me to look out the window at the dazzle of light on the water. Long thin strands of white lined the coast below us, and I could almost feel that sugar-fine sand between my toes. I clasped his hand in mine and watched the view tilt and shift as we began our descent to the airport.

God bless Debbie, I thought. Without Steve's sister, we never would have been able to break away. Debbie flew in from Oregon to take care of our animals and the house while we were gone, and I was deeply grateful. Steve's sister Mary was another lifesaver in my world—she and her husband R.J. had moved to Michigan to run our household while Steve had his heart operation. And of course his sister Susie had been my rock during the aftermath of the fire, and worked tirelessly to help me set up our office. Over the years I'd grown close to these women, who were just as strong, capable and intelligent as their brother. I loved them as if they were my own sisters, and I was incredibly grateful for all the support and love they'd shown us.

I snuggled deeper into my seat and checked my seat belt one more time. For the next seven days, we had only one job: Have Fun. Steve and Perry would play golf while Faye and I lay by the pool or sunned ourselves on the beach. The four of us would gather in the evenings to drink and eat good food by the water and watch the sunset.

Oh yeah, I thought. *I can handle that.*

The next morning I could hardly wait to run out of the hotel and wade into the sapphire blue water of the Gulf of Mexico. I wanted to feel hot sand between my toes, walk through the surf and soak off the hard Michigan calluses on my feet. I wanted to kick up a spray of salt water and watch it rain back into the sea in a dazzle of rainbows. It was all out there waiting for me, just a few feet away from our front door.

I phoned Perry and Faye and arranged to meet them in the lobby, then turned to Steve. "We're going for a walk on the beach—you want to come with us?"

He smoothed the front of his Sansabelt slacks. His golfing uniform never changed: Sansabelt slacks, polo shirts and sneakers. He ordered new slacks every year or two, and never let me get rid of any. He must have had a hundred shirts and a hundred pairs of slacks in his closet at home. I hated the polyester slacks and bought other blends for him, but he remained true to polyester.

"Perry's coming," I told him. "Faye too. We'll take it easy, I promise." I knew Steve had trouble walking more than a few hundred yards, even down here in the Florida warmth, but I hated to leave him in the hotel on our first morning of vacation.

Steve pulled on a polo shirt. "Perry and I have a ten o'clock tee time at Tiburon. That's enough for me. But don't forget my coffee in your travels."

I touched his shoulder. Ever since his heart surgery I couldn't stop touching him and clinging to him like a mother fussing over a newborn. I knew I was hovering, but I couldn't make myself stop. "Are you sure?"

He turned to look out the window at the clear blue sky. "Damn it, would you look at that. No clouds again. You women are just going to hate this."

I laughed and moved to the full-length mirror to check my reflection. Just an hour of sun the afternoon before had given my face a healthy glow. I had a new red two-piece bathing suit, and a sweet little beach wrap that hugged my hips.

Steve slipped his arm around my waist, and I leaned against him while we stood there for a moment, studying our reflection together. After a single day and night away from the business, the worry and frown lines on his face had melted, and he looked like the carefree man I'd fallen in love with twenty-three years ago.

My red bathing suit made a nice splash of color against the sparkling white of his shirt and slacks, and his gaze traveled up and down my figure.

"Whoa." He gave me a wink and raised his thumb.

My chest lifted at the note of approval in his voice. He wasn't the kind of man to make a romantic speech or spout compliments, but I knew he liked what he saw in the mirror. He was still gorgeous to me, still the same sexy Steve he'd always been, and I could not imagine a life without him. But his heart problems had rattled my faith in the long, sunny future I'd taken for granted. No more sex? Fine, I could deal with it. What

I couldn't deal with was the thought that his heart might stop beating.

He caught me staring at him, and I knew he read my mind. "Don't worry, Peep. I'll be here when you get back."

I gave him a squeeze. "We won't walk longer than an hour. You can wave to us from the balcony, okay?"

He gave me a little push. "Go on. You're burning daylight."

I shrugged and tried to pretend it didn't matter to me whether or not he stayed by himself. I gave him a kiss and left.

Two or three minutes later I was out on the beach, where the horizon stretched to Mexico, the sky was a serene, beautiful blue, and the sand reflected the brilliant light all around me. But I wasn't looking at the view. My eyes searched every balcony of the hotel until I saw Steve at the railing. He lifted his arm in a farewell salute.

I waved. My throat stung. I didn't want to leave, but I knew Perry and Faye were waiting for me a few yards down the beach. Steve turned and went back into the hotel room. I stood there and stared at the empty balcony for a few seconds, and then I walked down the beach without him.

The Kentucky Derby was televised that Saturday, and the four of us watched every minute of it while we sat in our favorite bar and ate pizza.

Not a heart-healthy choice! I screamed at Steve in my mind.

He read my expression and gave me his evil grin. "Ease up, Peep. We're on vacation."

When the race was over we headed over to Jimmy B's to

watch the sun sink into the ocean. Delicate pinks and blues and violets intensified to ruby and purple before the curtain of night closed out the show. We sat by the water, spellbound by the soft air, the lazy, sensual heat that saturated our cold Michigan bones, and swayed to a Jimmy Buffet tune as the guitarist crooned into a microphone. We sat there until the stars came out. Laughing. Telling jokes. Buying rounds of drinks. We watched an old man walk into the water, swim up and down along the shore, then jump out and run the beach. Steve pointed out another man in the bar who looked exactly like Jed Clampett from the Beverly Hillbillies. This guy danced like a lunatic for hours, no matter what music was playing. We were completely absorbed by the spectacle of the beach walkers, the drinkers, and the beautiful Cuban boys who hustled back and forth to bus the tables. Steve slipped hundred dollar bills to the bartender and our waitress, and they greeted us by name and made sure our glasses were always full.

The next morning when Faye, Perry and I finished our walk on the beach, we saw Steve waiting for us in the lobby, car keys dangling from his hand.

"*Vamanos,*" he said. "Let's take a field trip."

Whenever Steve decided to skip golf and go out with "the wives" for the day, he called it a field trip. I loved these trips. In the past we'd toured the Everglades, rented jet skis and even tried parasailing. We didn't bother to change clothes—we all followed Steve out to the parking lot and jumped in the car, ready for adventure.

After a forty mile drive we crossed a bridge to Marco Island and pulled up in front of a restaurant called Snook Inn. An open-air chickee bar hugged the water of the Marco River and the view opened out to the wide vista of the Gulf of Mexico. It looked like a classic old-Florida thatched bar and restaurant, and the smells coming from the barbecue were enough to make me swoon.

"How did you hear about this place?" I asked Steve.

"Spike told me." Spike was our favorite bartender at the hotel, a larger-than-life woman who had long blonde hair and an eastern accent.

They'd just started serving lunch. We ordered cocktails—a Virgin Mary for Steve, with pickled asparagus instead of celery—and full-octane Bloody Marys for the rest of us. We sat under the thatched roof of the bar while water slapped against the dock and dolphins played in the river so close to us we could see their smiles.

We ate every special on the menu. Perry had the Shrimp Denny: shrimp stuffed with scallops, wrapped in bacon, deep fried and served with hollandaise sauce.

"Artery- cloggers," Steve kidded him.

"You mind your own shrimp, I'll take care of these," Perry said.

Steve had the Shrimp Scorpion, which had a spicy-hot kick, served with raspberry sauce. Faye and I ate grouper fingers and fried clams, and we all tasted bites from each other's plates as we watched yachts, catamarans, trawlers and shrimp boats go by. Pelicans cruised the shoreline, gliding in unison in one long graceful line just a few inches above the water.

We sat there on the dock for hours. Steve had the old bright sparkle in his eyes, and I realized I'd missed that sparkle during the long slog after the fire, when both of us had been buried in work and insurance forms.

I stroked Steve's arm. "You'd live ten years longer if we spent our winters here where you could be warm."

He stretched his arms out and laced his hands behind his head. "Hell yeah, I could live like this. Golf every day. Eat like a king every night. What do you think, Peep? Maybe we should call the plant and tell them we got sunned in down here."

"I'm all for it," I said. "Too much sun to make it out of the driveway, for sure."

"Naples is nice," Perry said. "Bonita Springs? I could live there."

We lapsed back into silence. I knew we wouldn't move. Not now. Not unless we sold the business, and I knew Steve would never go for it. The business was his baby, and he wasn't about to let anybody else run it.

Two egrets swooped down on the dock just a few feet away from us, and we watched as they picked their way over the boards to the sign that said "Please Don't Feed the Birds."

"Look at that," Steve said. "Pete and Re-Pete." He tossed them each a piece of shrimp, and they caught the chunks in mid-air and wolfed them down, beaks pointed skyward.

When the guitarist began to sing a Willie Nelson tune, Steve nudged my foot with his.

Maybe I didn't treat you, quite as good as I should have . . . You were always on my mind.

Steve leaned over to whisper in my ear. "This is my song for you."

I nodded. I found it difficult to speak. I reached for his

hand and gave it a squeeze.

We were all quiet for a few minutes after the song. We leaned back to drink in the infinite horizon, the sound of waves lapping against the dock and the soft hoot of mourning doves in the coconut palms. Everything Steve and I had been through in the past twenty years had brought us here to this one perfect moment. It was beautiful. We'd succeeded at everything we'd set out to do.

Isn't this enough? I asked myself.

I knew it should be enough. But the beauty filled me with a fierce longing I couldn't put into words.

Steve looked around the table and gave us his bad-boy smile. "I wonder what all the poor people are doing tonight?"

Faye and Perry traded a look and shook their heads.

My life with Steve had shaped me, and most of the time it felt like I didn't even exist without him. Most of the time that didn't seem like such a terrible thing. He'd molded my life to fit his, and I loved the life he'd given me. He was always onstage, always the capital-B-Boss and the life of the party wherever he went. I was the quiet one, the stage manager in the background, there to help him make decisions and take care of the tasks he hated. I was fine with that. I was good at it. He'd given me the chance to get good at it, and I loved the life we shared at work.

But now I wanted to stop. Why were we both killing ourselves with work, instead of enjoying the time that remained? Money didn't matter. Money was the last thing that mattered. I wanted to sell the company and enjoy a quiet life with my husband, away from the commotion of running a business. I wanted to travel with him, relax with him, putter around the house, plant a garden and watch sports on TV with him.

How many times had Steve told me he would die young?

How many years do we have left?

❧ Chapter Fourteen ❧

By July 1999, the aneurysm on Steve's aorta was big enough to need surgery, so we scheduled it for the Friday of Labor Day weekend at the Cleveland Clinic.

No one could tell me how long the procedure would last, and after our last experience with surgery, I knew it would probably be another marathon in the waiting room. I'd been through this before, but it didn't make it any easier to sit there and wait while the hours crawled by.

This is what hell must be like, I thought. Fluorescent lights. Green carpet. Three vending machines. No windows. I knew exactly how many minutes there were between the refrigeration cycles of the Pepsi machine. I counted the ceiling tiles: eight hundred and sixty-four. Then I counted them again. I held every magazine in the rack and pretended to read, but I was too anxious to read, so I turned the pages instead. If I forced myself to go slowly and stared at each page before I turned it, it used up three or four seconds. It took forty-two minutes to finish scanning each page in each magazine in the stack, and then I went back to the first magazine and started the process all over again.

The surgery lasted eleven hours.

When they finally called my name and told me I could see my husband, I nearly ran down the hallway toward his room.

As I approached his bed, Steve began to weep.

What have they done to you? I thought. I leaned down to touch my forehead to his. "You're okay, buddy, everything is okay. I'm here now." I stroked his face, smoothed his hair and kissed his cheeks while he fought to control himself. The last time I'd seen him cry had been two years earlier, after the fire burned our business to rubble and ash.

His breath jerked, and when he finally spoke his voice was hoarse with rage. "They gave me a drug. It paralyzed me. I couldn't move a muscle, couldn't talk, but I was awake, and my eyes were open. This fucking doctor, he shoved a tube into my nostril. It was supposed to go down my throat to my stomach."

"Why?" I asked. "What was it for?"

"They said they had to drain the fluid in my stomach after the surgery. But the tube didn't go down my throat, Peep." For a moment he couldn't speak. He pressed his lips together tight, then took a deep breath. "The tube coiled up and twisted inside my mouth. It nearly choked me."

I closed my eyes, and pain bloomed in the center of my chest. I did not want to hear this.

"I couldn't move! I couldn't talk! The goddamn drug had me paralyzed. I couldn't tell them what was happening. I was gagging on the fucking tube, and they kept shoving it in."

The door opened, and we both looked up to see the head of the intensive care unit, enter the room with an entourage of interns. They all gathered around Steve's bed and stared down at him. The doctors appeared well-rested, well-fed and immaculate in their white coats. They smelled like soap, cologne and hair gel, and they looked at Steve with an air of detached pity.

Just looking at them made me want to punch somebody.

The doctor consulted the chart before he walked around the bed to pick up an eight inch long plastic tube with a silicone mouthpiece from the nightstand.

"Mr. Milks, you need to show me you know how to use the lung exerciser that your doctor provided for you." He lifted the lung exerciser and held it up so everyone in the room could see it.

Steve glared at him. "I know how to use the goddamn lung exerciser."

"You may think you know how to use it." He turned to smile at the interns who stood behind him. "But you need to show me you can use it." He leaned over and tried to insert the mouthpiece into Steve's mouth.

Steve grabbed the lung exerciser from the doctor's hand. "Peep? Will you tell this fucking asshole that if he doesn't leave right now, I'm going to throw his fucking lung exerciser out the window?"

"You'd better do what he says," I said to the doctor. "I can't control him when he's like this."

The doctor took a step back. "We need to make sure you can clear the anesthetic from your lungs, that's all—"

Steve pointed to the door. "Get out!" He hefted the lung exerciser in his palm and faked a pass at him.

The head of intensive care flinched, hustled towards the door, with six interns hot on his heels.

As the days passed, Steve's strength and stamina slowly improved. Eight days after the surgery, he was finally strong enough to come back home. As soon as he limped through our front door, he went to the phone to call the plant.

"I'm back," he told Larry. "Peep will have to drive me, but I'll be at work tomorrow morning."

You just had surgery, I thought. *Why can't you slow down for once in your life and let yourself heal?* I was terrified he'd push himself until he dropped.

But as the days trickled by, it was clear he was stronger than he'd been before the surgery. His doctors not only repaired the aneurysm but they also performed bypass surgery on his groin arteries, which meant he could walk without pain in his legs for the first time in four or five years. Eventually he was able to walk a quarter mile down our driveway and back without too much effort. He'd limp by the time he got back to the house, but before the surgery he couldn't walk half that distance.

For a few years, his circulation flowed well, and life seemed as smooth and sweet as cream poured from a pitcher. Steve was always full of plans to improve the landscaping at home, and he wanted a big lawn. I pulled garden hoses around the yard all summer to keep the grass seed wet. When the grass was finally thick enough, we mowed it with a little Toro mower. It wasn't long before we bought a Grasshopper mower with a five-foot cut, a John Deere tractor with a mower deck attachment, and a sickle mower that Steve could haul around with the John Deere.

Steve kept extending the borders of the lawn until it eventually took us ten to twelve hours to mow the whole yard. Even with all this equipment, the mowing consumed our lives during the summer.

One afternoon while on a trip to Florida, Perry, Faye, Steve and I stopped at a Circle K station to buy some gas. While Steve filled the tank, a truck with a flatbed trailer pulled up next to him. Steve glanced over at the trailer, then stared at its cargo. Looming over his head was the Toro Groundsmaster 4700-D with seven mowing decks and a twelve foot cut. It looked like something out of a science fiction movie, an octopus with seven tentacles and a throne in the center. It was the ultimate mowing machine, the Cadillac of mowers.

Steve drew closer to it and stared at that mower like a man who'd just fallen in love. "Look at that!" he said to Perry. "I've got to have one of those."

Perry looked doubtful. "Thing must cost a fortune."

Steve reached up to stroke the finish on one of the octagonal mowing decks. "If the driver hasn't sold it yet, I'm going to buy it right now and have it trucked back to Michigan."

Perry laughed and shook his head. "You are not."

"You watch." Steve went over to make his pitch to the driver, who shook his head and told him the mower was already sold.

Steve talked about that mower the whole way home, and when he went back to work the next day he checked with his equipment dealers and found the mower was offered by Spartan Distributors in Auburn Hills, Michigan.

The following Friday afternoon they brought the mower out to the house. Usually Steve acted like Mr. Cool, but when they unloaded the mower he bounded toward the driver and his assistant, took the roll from his front pocket and peeled off a couple of hundred dollar bills for each of them.

The delivery man told us what all the levers were for, how to lift the decks, and how to shift between fast and slow speeds.

Steve nudged me with his elbow. "Come on Peep, get on it and try it out."

I backed away. "You're crazy if you think I'm getting on that mower first without knowing anything about it. You try it out. Then you can show me how to run it."

Finally Steve climbed up on the mower and slid into the driver's seat with a serious man-behind-the-wheel look, but his eyes were dancing with the thrill of it. He drove up and down the driveway, his face lit up with the pleasure of running the machine. He pulled out on the lawn, dropped all seven mowing decks down, pushed the switch to make the blades run and mowed a couple of twelve-foot strips.

The machine moved slowly, quietly, and it hugged the ground like a limousine. In the wake of its blades the lawn looked manicured as a putting green. The sweet smell of fresh-cut grass filled the air, and I itched with the desire to get up on the throne and try out the mower myself.

When he got off the mower, Steve looked at me, his eyes shining. "It's a hell of a sled, Peep. You're going to love mowing with this baby."

Feeling nervous, I mounted the throne and stared at the tentacles of the mowing decks that surrounded me. There were lots of levers, and no lever to reverse, just a pedal next to the gas pedal that reversed the mower. I was petrified of stepping on the wrong pedal. The first few swipes I made, I didn't lower all the decks. I thought I might hit something.

"Go on," Steve yelled over the noise of the engine. "Set 'em down."

As I settled myself behind the wheel, I finally levered the mowing decks down. It was a really comfortable ride, and I could adjust the seat forward to fit my height. Most mower manufacturers don't seem to have women in mind when they design mowers, but this was the queen of all lawnmowers. The machine purred under me, and I felt elegant and comfortable as if I were floating around the yard in an easy chair.

On Monday we wrote the company a check for fifty-three thousand dollars.

That lawnmower cost us more than our first house.

Whenever I gave Steve a hard time about spending too much on a piece of equipment after that, he'd say "It's cheaper than the lawnmower."

He used that statement a lot.

The business continued to flourish, and by 2002 we'd sold over two million fans. We expanded to fill the demand, and added five thousand square feet of office space, fourteen thousand square feet of warehouse space, fourteen thousand square feet for the production area, and half a million dollars' worth of presses to run our parts.

Steve loved spreading the wealth. We gave jobs to every friend and family member who wanted to work at the plant. Steve was a father figure to many of our seventy-five employees, and there was usually a steady parade through his office as they came to him for advice, encouragement or help with their problems.

Our rising income allowed us to give away cars, cash, land, furniture, vehicles, vacations and luxuries we never dreamed we could afford when we were just starting out. We set up college funds for our grandsons Shea and Seth and several of our nieces and nephews. After our grandson Stephen turned eighteen, we bought a new Ford Focus and dropped the keys to the car in the bottom of his Christmas stocking.

The neighbors up the street from us lost their house to a fire, and although we didn't know them well, we drove past the blackened timbers of their home every morning on the way to work. Even through our closed car window, I could smell the acrid burnt-wood stink of smoke. It brought back a stark reminder of our own disaster.

One morning I turned to Steve as we drove past the burned lot. "Can I write them a check tonight?"

He didn't even hesitate. "Make it a fat one."

That night I wrote them a check for five thousand dollars.

In 2003 Steve flew in a Citation 5 jet and absolutely loved it.

He sidled up to me the next day at work and sat on the edge of my desk. "Peep, you're going to love the convenience of our own jet. We'll save so much time! No waiting around in an airport."

Rain was drumming on the roof, and bare willow branches thrashed the window of my office. It was dark as night outside, even though it was only three in the afternoon. I was in the middle of calculating the figures for the week's payroll, and it took me a minute to disengage my mind from the computer monitor on my desk.

I leaned back in my chair and peered at Steve over the top of my glasses. "I don't mind waiting in airports. As soon as I walk in the door, I know I'm off duty."

"The delays," he groaned. "Security, lines for checking luggage! I hate that shit." He picked up a rubber band from my desk and stretched it with his thumbs until it snapped away and fell in the corner.

I folded my arms across my chest and raised an eyebrow.

He looked at me like I was a safe he was trying to crack. "Peep, I swear, if we get this jet, you'll never regret it."

"You already own a backhoe, a tractor, a bulldozer, a dump truck, a Bobcat—" I held up the fingers of one hand and counted them off. "A gigantic vacuum system container to hose up your grass clippings. .."

"We *need* a jet, Peep. It'll be good for business."

"…a fully restored 1964 Plymouth Sport Fury, a 2002 Thunderbird—."

"That's your baby," he snorted.

"… two Mercury Mountaineers, a 2003 Lincoln…"

"But this jet is the ultimate convenience! We drive to the hanger, get out of the car, step in the jet and take off, right out of the hangar! No waiting, no lines, no hassle. No drips, no runs, no errors. It's perfect."

I gave him a look. "Don't you think we have enough vehicles, Stephen?"

He hiked himself off the desk. "Just think about it. That's all I ask."

As he walked out to the hallway, I overheard Perry call out to him. "So? You convince her yet?"

"I haven't got it kicked in the river," Steve said. "But I got it dragged to the bank."

After a year of listening to him moan about the jet, I finally gave in. In November 2004 Steve signed the papers, and from then on we flew in the Citation whenever we felt like traveling.

One night in September 2005, I noticed Steve was holding his head above his eye. For the past few months I'd been worried about his left eye. There was a subtle difference in it, a lack of focus that disturbed me every time I looked at it.

"You have a headache, buddy?" I asked him.

"I'm trying to get the blinker light to shut off!" He shouted as if I were a hundred yards away from him, instead of sitting on the other end of the couch with his feet in my lap.

The hair prickled on my arms, and I made my voice soft to try to calm him. "What blinker light?"

"The one that keeps going off," he yelled.

I moved his feet from my lap and stood up. "I'm calling the doctor."

"*NO!*" he bellowed. "I'm not going to any goddamn doctor."

In my heart I knew we should go to the emergency room, but Steve grew angry every time I brought it up, and I didn't dare push it.

Two weeks later, in October 2005, I went to St. Louis, Missouri to help my mother while she had lung surgery. It went well, although there were some frightening moments when I didn't think she was going to make it. I called Steve two or three times a day to update him and make sure he was okay. After I'd been gone almost two weeks, I missed him desperately.

A couple of days before I was due to return, I called him

again. "You surviving without me up there?"

"I don't feel so great," he said. "I'm having some trouble breathing."

He didn't sound good. He wheezed as if he were out of breath from running to the phone. But Steve didn't run anywhere, ever. I felt a cold trickle of alarm slide down my spine, and fumbled for words. "What happened? When did you first notice it?"

"I went to Meijer's to pick up a prescription, and when I got home I couldn't breathe."

"But … you're okay now?"

"I don't know. I haven't been eating too well since you left."

I squeezed the phone. "I'll be home soon."

Two days later, Steve flew down on the company jet to pick me up. As soon as he emerged from the jet, I could see he looked thinner, especially in his face.

I hugged him and felt his ribs under his coat. "You look so skinny." I couldn't stop touching him.

"I probably lost some weight," he admitted. "I've been living on cheese and peaches since you left."

The simplest actions winded him. Buckling his seat belt, taking off his jacket, lifting a magazine—any tiny movement left him sounding out of breath.

The next day I made an appointment for Steve to go in and see the doctor, and this time he didn't object. When we returned home after a long day at the office, Steve went into the living room to lie down on the couch.

"You want something to drink?" I asked him as I headed

to the kitchen.

There was no answer. I ran back into the living room and saw Steve gasping on the couch. His chest rose as he took little sips of air, but he couldn't take a deep breath. His face flushed from the effort to breathe, and he struggled to sit up. I helped him stand and walked him over to the La-Z-Boy. After a few minutes of sitting vertically, he could breathe a little more easily.

It was obvious that something was wrong, and I knew it was bad. I just couldn't look directly at it yet.

Steve and I sat in Dr. Ron's office and tried not to look at each other. We examined all the pictures on the wall, checked out all the knickknacks, pens, pictures and flowers on Ron's desk. We stared at the clock. We looked at everything in that office but each other.

Dr. Ron walked in and sat behind his desk.

"It's cancer," he said quietly. "You have a tumor in your lungs."

Steve looked at me and tried to smile. "Here comes the toe tag."

I pressed my lips together, stared at him and fought to keep from crying. The silence grew into an abyss I couldn't cross.

Dr. Ron cleared his throat. "I think it's a type of cancer you can fight. I'd like to refer you to a specialist who has had some good results with this kind of tumor. But we should probably do a few more tests, to make sure the cancer hasn't spread."

I stared at Dr. Ron's mouth as he went on talking about the new chemo treatment his colleague had devised. By the time we left the office, I was convinced we could beat this. We'd come too far to give in to a bunch of greedy cells that had the nerve to take up residence and multiply in Steve's lungs.

On the way home Steve was quiet, and stared out the passenger window with a faraway look in his eyes.

We rented the video "Weekend at Bernie's" that night. It was one of Steve's favorite comedies, about a couple of bumbling young insurance executives who discover the dead body of their boss "Bernie" at his beach house. The two young men do everything they can to convince people that Bernie is still alive, so they can go on living the high life at the beach house. Wherever they go, they deck out the corpse with sunglasses and a hat, hold it in an upright position and take Bernie with them.

While we watched the video, I snuggled next to Steve on the couch and helped myself to the bowl of popcorn in his lap. "If you die on me, I'm going to prop you up and take you with me everywhere."

He smiled. "Might get a bit ripe in the summer."

"Then I'll have to take you to the taxidermist, get you stuffed. You'll be my Bernie."

"Bernie" became a steady joke between us, and we told the kids we planned to have Steve stuffed so we could take him along on all our family vacations. They laughed. We were desperate for any crumb of humor we could find in the situation, and I was determined not to give in to despair or sorrow in front of Steve.

On November 22, Dr. Ron's nurse called. She said the doctor wanted us to come to the office after hours so he could give us the results of the scans he'd completed.

Steve took the phone from my hand. "No, Cathy. We're not

coming in for another office visit. Just put Ron on the phone and let him give it to me straight."

Cathy transferred the phone to Dr. Ron, and I heard his voice crackle over the line.

"Steve? Is Penny with you?"

"She's here," Steve wrapped an arm around my waist, and I stood close to him and leaned in to listen.

"I'm afraid the cancer has metastasized. It's in the brain."

My knees turned to jelly. I crumpled to the floor by Steve, and he patted me on the head while he went on talking to Dr. Ron. How could I contain this news and stay sane? Dr. Ron had just handed me a burning coal that I was supposed to hold in my bare hands for the rest of my life. I didn't want to cry. I didn't want to feel this jagged hurt. I clung to Steve's leg and stared numbly toward the grief that lay ahead.

Steve's first radiation treatment to his head was on December 27. We were both apprehensive about it, but it wasn't too bad. That night I massaged Vitamin E oil and aloe on his scalp, forehead, temples, and ears. After each radiation treatment, he lost a little more hair, but not all of it, and his scalp didn't burn.

On our way to and from the hospital, Steve and I talked about our lives together and how we started out. We giggled at some of our funny memories; the night we drove out by the pond to sing along with Jimmy Buffet on the radio and backed over the well. The day he lifted me up in the bucket of the backhoe to place a wreath on the house, realizing too late my fear of heights. I loved the luxury of having him all to myself, until he started listing the things he wanted me to do if he didn't make it.

I wasn't about to discuss the possibility of his dying while I was trying to drive in Detroit in four lanes of traffic at seventy-five miles an hour.

"You're going to be fine," I told him.

"Yeah, yeah," he said. "But you need to know I talked to Dave. I changed the partnership agreement between us and put your name on the contract, instead of mine. You have the tie-breaking vote if there's any debate with Dave."

"*What?* Why did you do that?"

"You're the CEO now, Peep. I'm giving you control of the company."

My throat stung with emotion. It was a mark of his faith in me, and I was touched by his confidence. But I didn't want to have this conversation with him. I couldn't picture his office empty, his desk unused. How could Steve die? He was only sixty-five years old! I couldn't imagine him dead, closed up in a box, buried in a hole in the ground, or burned to ashes. It was impossible.

"I'm still not sure you're going to have enough money after I die," he said.

His words chilled me to the core. I couldn't imagine a life without Steve, and this kind of talk brought me to the edge of a despair I didn't want to contemplate.

"You could live a good long time after I'm dead," he said. "You'll probably marry again. You should be married, Peep. I want you to be happy. But you need plenty of money no matter what."

"Enough!" I snapped. "If I'm president of the company, I can pay myself the same thing you pay yourself." *Stephen, I will have enough money.*

He stopped talking and looked at me, and I could almost see the light bulb go on over his head as he realized I could take care of myself, no matter what happened.

His blue eyes sparkled with affection, and his voice was soft. "Damn straight. You'll be fine."

Steve grew thinner and weaker from the chemo and radiation treatments for his brain tumor. He spent entire days upstairs lying in bed, watching sports on TV and making phone calls. When he was asleep, I kept running upstairs to make sure he was still breathing. When he was awake, he wanted me on call, ready to scoot up and down the stairs to bring him whatever he wanted. He loved soaking in the whirlpool tub because the bubbling jets made his body feel better, but he couldn't stand on his own after he came out of the tub. I had to lift him out, dry him and apply cream to his skin—a process that took well over an hour and exhausted both of us.

One Saturday morning I went up and down the stairs at least eighteen times in one hour. My mind felt thick as fudge. I tried to remember how many times I'd climbed the stairs since I'd woken up that day, and lost count at forty. I trudged back down to the kitchen and slopped berries and milk into the blender to make him a strawberry shake. It was hard to find food he could tolerate, and the flesh seemed to disappear from his bones, no matter how hard I tried to tempt him with soft, easily digestible food.

Steve called down the stairs. "Peep, I need a nausea pill. My stomach's in knots."

It took me a minute to ponder the assortment of pill bottles on the kitchen counter before I could pick out the bottle with his nausea pills.

It was empty. I'd forgotten to refill the prescription.

A fresh wave of fatigue crashed over me as I realized I'd have to drive to the pharmacy. "I'll be right back," I called up the stairs. "I need to fill the prescription."

I drove through lunchtime traffic in a cold drizzle. The windshield wipers slapped away sleet, and the traffic lights and the faces of pedestrians blurred in the wet glass. A lump of grief weighed on my chest like a stone. What would I do if Steve didn't get better and I had to go on like this? My life had become impossible. I was living on catnaps, snatching sleep whenever I could, but it wasn't enough.

The Meijers parking lot was crammed with cars. Inside the market, I stood in line for thirty minutes to pick up the pills and pay for them. I could hardly keep my eyes open on the drive back home, and when I finally walked in the door and faced the staircase, it looked like Everest.

I dragged myself up the eleven steps and pasted a smile on my face as I entered our bedroom.

"Did you remember to get me any peaches?" he asked.

My head snapped back. *No!* I thought. *No, I didn't get your goddamned fucking peaches!* Anger boiled up in me and flooded my face with heat.

I threw the bottle of pills on the floor. "Do you know how many times I've run up these stairs for you today? You run me off my feet all day long! I do all this for you and you never even acknowledge it! You never say 'thank you, Peep' or 'good job,

Peep!' You just take me for granted, and I'm sick of it!"

Crazed with fatigue, crazed with fear, crazed by the dark sword of cancer that hung suspended over our lives, I wanted *out*.

Steve opened his mouth to speak, but I roared over him. "I have spent my whole life taking care of you!" I yelled. "I can't do it anymore! I'm tired!"

He stared at me. There was a flicker of fear in his eyes, and that wariness broke my heart.

I covered my mouth with both hands. My husband was sick, he had cancer, and I had just yelled at him because he'd asked me for a can of peaches.

What kind of monster am I?

I sank down on the bed, dropped my elbows to my knees and leaned forward to hide my face in my hands. "I'm sorry, Stephen. I'm so scared. I'm scared all the time." I shook my head. "I sit up at night while you sleep and I watch you breathe to make sure you don't stop breathing. It seems like I never sleep anymore. I can't go on like this."

He pushed away the sheets and blankets and moved toward me. Soon I felt his arms wrap around my waist, and I turned blindly toward the warmth of his embrace and hung on tight. He hugged me with all his strength he had left.

"You know I love you, don't you?" His voice cracked. "You're my crutch, Peep. You're my crutch because you're stronger than me. You hold me up and I can lean on you."

I kept my eyes squeezed shut. "I don't know how to get through this."

He kissed my cheek with infinite tenderness. "We'll get

through it." He pressed his lips to my hair and whispered "It's going to be tough on you, Peep."

When I opened my eyes I saw him look at me with a strange, tender, compassionate expression, as if he understood everything I'd felt and would feel before this was over.

He stared out the window, and his eyes shone with tears. "When I'm gone… I'll find a way to make sure you know I love you. Because I do, Peep. I love you now, and I will love you forever, and forever after that."

A few days later Steve was admitted to the hospital for acute pancreatitis. His breathing became more and more labored, and a lung specialist tested him and discovered his right diaphragm was paralyzed. No one knew what caused the paralysis, and no one knew how to fix it. After the chemo and radiation treatments, he was already so weak he had trouble standing up at the sink to brush his teeth.

On March 1, 2006 they admitted him to intensive care.

Steve's back began to hurt him more and more, and after he'd spent a few days in the ICU, we requested a special bed to ease the pain. The bed had electronic sensors that inflated the mattress every few minutes, then deflated to shift the pressure points and offer him relief from long periods of immobility. The bed itself seemed to breathe: one long inhale was followed by a long exhale, and the cycle repeated itself every two or three minutes.

Steve found it more and more difficult to breathe. He had to wear a mask strapped around his head while oxygen blew through a hose into his nose and mouth. God, he hated that contraption. The nurses strapped his arms down at night so he wouldn't tear it off in his sleep.

One day he clawed at the mask and yelled "God damn it, God damn it!"

I yelled right along with him, "You're right! God damn it! It's not fair but you need this mask to breathe!"

He sank back against the pillows, exhausted. A moment later he held out his arms for me and when I leaned in to hug him, he clung to me tightly. His voice was nearly gone, barely a whisper. "I'm not going to make it, Peep."

I took his face in my hands. "You will make it. I can't lose you."

He shook his head and fell back against the pillows, exhausted.

I smoothed the hair back from his forehead, kissed him and closed my eyes. I struggled every day to avoid crying in front of Steve. That night, though, I couldn't manage it.

When he could no longer talk, he wrote me a note. The writing was tiny, a barely readable scrawl. The note said "Why can't I breathe?"

He gasped for air all day and all night, day after day, night after night.

During the nights, I slept on a mat on the floor by his bed. The room reeked of antiseptic, but underneath that astringent smell there was a musky odor of decay. After Steve had been in the ICU for almost a week, Stephanie spent nights so I could have a break, and we slept together on the mat, butt to butt. She tended him while I rested, and I took care of him while she slept. Every few hours we used a suction hose to clear the phlegm from his mouth to keep him from choking.

At night I listened to the bed hiss as it inflated and deflated. Nurses walked in and out of the room every hour to take another blood draw or adjust his medications. I snatched a few minutes of sleep whenever I could, but fear kept me awake most of the time.

In the morning I stared out the window that overlooked the parking lot. Beyond the acres of cars there were some trees, but the trees seemed far away. I couldn't remember what it was like to live a normal life in the outside world. My world had shrunk to the space by Steve's bed, between the IV lines and the valve in the wall that supplied the oxygen for his mask.

After Steve had been in intensive care for eight days, one of his doctors knocked on the door and peeked in. "Mrs. Milks? I'd like to talk to you for a moment."

"Of course," I said. "Come in."

The doctor closed the door behind him, leaned against the wall and put his hands in his pockets. He regarded me with kind, patient eyes. "Your husband can't breathe without the ventilator. You know that, don't you?"

"I know." My voice felt rusty. My tongue felt like fur. I'd been wearing the same clothes for three days, and I couldn't remember the last time I'd slept for more than an hour.

The doctor stared out the window. "Do you realize he'll never be able to breathe without the machine?"

I gripped the armrest of my chair. "I—no, I didn't know that."

He shifted his gaze from the window to study my face. "Did he tell you he wanted to be on life support?"

"No," I said quietly. "He would have hated that idea."

He lifted his chin toward the ventilator. "Then we need your permission to take off the mask, and release him from the machine."

My insides began to shake. Perspiration formed on my upper lip and I tried to take a deep breath. *I can't do this*, I thought. *I don't want to do this.* Acid rose in the back of my throat and I swallowed to force it back down. I desperately wanted someone—anyone—to tell me what the right choice was. Give up? Unplug him from life support? Or keep him hooked up to it, no matter what?

I looked up at the doctor. "If your wife were hooked up to that mask, would you take her off the machine?"

He didn't hesitate. "If she were suffering the way your husband is suffering? Absolutely. Yes, I would take her off the machine."

"Thank you," I whispered. "I appreciate your candor."

He held me with his gaze and waited for an answer.

I reached out to hold Steve's hand in mine. There was no response when I squeezed his fingers. He hadn't spoken or opened his eyes in three days. It broke my heart to see the bruised skin around the oxygen mask he hated. His forehead was lined with misery, even in his sleep, and he'd lost forty pounds since he'd been diagnosed. The body I'd loved for so long had wasted away until there was nothing left but a husk.

I looked up at the doctor. "All right. Let's do this thing."

The doctor nodded. "Once we remove the mask, it may

take a while for him to die. You have some time. You can call his family."

"Thank you." My throat closed.

The doctor left the room.

Stevie and Stephanie were both with me when the nurse came in that evening to take Steve off the respirator.

"Are you ready?" the nurse asked us.

We looked at each other. The kids looked as frightened as I felt. I took both of them by the hand, swallowed the lump in my throat and nodded.

The nurse hooked up an IV morphine drip for Steve. Gently, tenderly, she removed the ventilator mask from his face. His breathing continued, shallow but steady. There was a small spasm in his arm, but otherwise he slept peacefully.

During the next few hours, the kids and I spoke in low murmurs about Steve, about his illness and the past few days. As the night wore on, we talked about the way he used to be, and told stories about happier times. Sledding down the hill in back of our townhouse in New York. Our trips to the candy store. Stephanie laughed as she recalled the night she and her girlfriends came over, every one of them dressed to the nines in mini-skirts, push-up bras and tube tops, ready for a big night in Saginaw. Steve went upstairs, came down with four of his shirts and made them cover themselves before they left the house. I told them about our wedding day, and how Steve insisted on stopping by an RV dealership in Jackson after the ceremony. Steve joked with the owner and told him we'd just gotten married.

We watched his chest rise and fall. For an hour or two

I got right up on the bed with him, talked to him, wiped his brow with a wet washcloth, held his face in my hands and kissed his cheeks.

He continued to sleep peacefully.

In the morning Stephanie and I stood by the bed and we both leaned over to caress his face. "Good morning, Stephen," I said. "It's nine a.m., March ninth, 2006."

His eyes flew open.

Oh! I thought. *Come back to us!*

His eyes were bright blue, like windows to the sky, a bottomless, beautiful blue. There was no pain in his gaze. Only love. He radiated peace, and I felt a great calm float down over me.

Steve closed his eyes. He took a breath, and let it go.

We waited in silence. His chest was still. For a moment the world felt hushed, expectant, like a suspended breath before the curtain opens in a theater. My skin tingled everywhere.

He's gone, I thought.

My body was numb, but the tingling remained. I slid one hand around the back of his neck and placed my other hand over his heart. There was no movement there, no rising of his chest. No heartbeat. His face was peaceful.

He's gone.

I felt fragile as a teacup falling through space. Soon I would shatter. But not yet. *Not yet.*

A nurse came in the room and approached the bed. I moved my hand so she could listen for his heartbeat with her stethoscope. She turned off the heart monitor, and I turned my face away when she did that.

I was still numb. Still falling. Still caught between the world I'd known with Steve and the world that waited for me without him.

The nurse dropped the stethoscope in her pocket, walked toward the door and hesitated on the threshold as she looked back at me. "Take all the time you need."

She closed the door softly behind her, and Stephanie and Stevie stared up at me.

I wasn't thinking. I couldn't think. I couldn't feel my own body, and I couldn't wrap my mind around the fact that Steve was dead. I didn't comprehend this would be the last time I would see him. I didn't know what I was supposed to do next. I was still in shock, still falling, still waiting for Steve to wake up and tell me what to do.

Suddenly the mattress began to inflate, and Steve's body rose toward the ceiling as the air compressor whirred underneath the bed.

It startled us. The kids and I took a step away from the bed. Then Stephanie darted forward, reached down and switched off the compressor.

As soon as she switched off the power, the mattress began to deflate, and Steve's body sank into it as if he'd fallen into quicksand. The mattress material began to envelop him.

Her brother panicked. "No! You need to turn it back on!"

Stephanie scrambled to turn the compressor on, and the mattress began to inflate again.

Steve's body rose toward the ceiling as the mattress coils filled with air. After he was lifted nine or ten inches, his chest expanded, and his arms flopped to his side.

We stepped back and Stephanie looked at me, her eyes wide. I stared back at her. At the exact same moment, we both said "Bernie!"

I started to laugh. I couldn't help it.

Stephanie and I tried to avert our eyes from each other, but the sound of her snorts and smothered giggles and the sight of her red face set me off again. I knew it was terrible to laugh at that moment. I turned away so I wouldn't have to see her, but I could hear her chortling, and the desire to laugh rose up in me like a sneeze. I bent over, clutched my knees and sucked in air, but I couldn't hold it. I let the air rush out of me in one long giggling cascade of laughter.

Stevie looked shocked. Then he smiled and shook his head and laughed a little too, but Stephanie and I were gone, over the edge, and we both laughed until tears streamed down our faces. I could hardly breathe. My whole body let loose and I started to pee. Once the floodgate opened, I couldn't stop, and warm urine ran down both my legs. I didn't care. My fear slid away in that moment. That familiar squeeze of terror, or pressure, or guilt—it was gone. My shoulders shook and jiggled and the tension ebbed from me like a toppled wave being pulled back to sea. It just didn't seem to matter anymore that there was a growing puddle between my feet.

When Stephanie saw the water on the floor she covered her mouth with her hands and whooped through her fingers. "Get a mop, clean up in aisle three!"

I sank into a chair, overwhelmed by an odd relief, as though I'd just escaped from a prison I'd been living in for months. Yes, I was tired, I was past the point of exhaustion, but Steve's suffering had finally ended, and that left me lighter.

I shook my head, wiped my eyes and looked up at the ceiling. "You've got to love this, Stephen."

Was he here? Was he aware of us? If he were floating above the hospital walls that had held him captive for too long, flying into the blue sunny hereafter ... I thought he might be laughing too.

Are you watching us, buddy?

I hoped so.

Epilogue

Epilogue

It's hot. A brilliant blue July day, already warm at nine a.m. on this Saturday morning. The birds sing in the trees while I walk out the front door in my pajamas, stretch my arms overhead and contemplate the lawn. The grass is shaggy, lush, in need of a clipping. I walk toward the pole barn in my bare feet, and think about the way I was barefoot when I jumped in Steve's car thirty-four years ago and left Missouri for Michigan.

Inside the pole barn, shafts of light filter through the windows, and the smells of earth and grass and machine oil hang in the air. My gardening tools are neatly arranged on hooks in pegboard, and a variety of mowers and tillers are parked along the north wall. With the heel of my hand I tap the garage door opener, and the door to the middle bay scrolls open to reveal the Toro Groundsmaster.

I climb on board, settle myself on the throne, and turn the key to the first position to warm up the engine. After a minute or two, the mower is ready to start.

It fires up with a puff of smoke and the familiar smell of diesel fuel. Funny how this smell reminds me of summertime, and the sweet lazy feeling of the weekend, when I have the glory of Saturday and Sunday ahead of me.

The mower is low on fuel, so I pull over to the diesel tank and fill it up. I never let the fuel get below one quarter of a tank. Steve always said "Never run a diesel out of fuel," and I hear his words every time I'm tempted to mow with less fuel than I should.

Once she's gassed up, I'm ready to go. Since I've been doing this for seven years, I know how to make the striping run in the prettiest pattern. I start on the bank of the west side of the pond and mow straight south towards the entrance to the property. This first swipe sets the pattern for the whole yard.

Time loses all meaning when I'm riding the mower. I do my best thinking out here, but mostly I like to let my mind wander. The air this morning has a shine to it, and the buttery light shimmers on the dew. Oak leaves rustle in the breeze. A kingfisher preens on a dead branch by the side of the pond, and a leaf falls toward me, spinning through the air until it kisses the surface of the water.

The mower rumbles underneath me, leaving perfect stripes of clipped lawn in its wake. A drop of sweat rolls down my back as the sun rises and bakes my skin. The velvet stretch of Kentucky bluegrass slopes directly down to the pond in an unbroken expanse of green. There are no dandelions, no crabgrass to mar the emerald carpet that stretches out like a fairway ahead of me.

What would it be like to live in a warm state? I wonder. *Florida, maybe, or North Carolina. Or I could spend winters here and travel all summer. Go out west and see Yellowstone. I could go all the way to Australia.*

As I make the turn under the weeping willow I think about the way Steve made fun of me when I planted the tree on Arbor Day, back when we bought the property.

"It looks like a stick!" he said. "Why bother planting a twig like that? You'll never get it to grow."

The willow stands fifteen feet tall and twelve feet wide now, and its branches form a lush curtain of green that waves in the breeze. Every time I mow under it I smile.

"What do you think of my stick tree now, Stephen?" I ask out loud.

I remember how I used to come home from work before he did, strip off my suit coat, kick off my pumps, peel off my pantyhose in the garage and step up on the mower. I'd warm up the engine on the Toro, aim for the lawn and start cutting. When Steve pulled in the driveway he would smile, step out of the car and wave me over to him. I'd hop off the mower and give him a welcome-home kiss.

It always felt so good to hug him and kiss him. I miss that tight hug. It makes me ache sometimes, how much I miss him.

My yard is one of the few places where I can relax and unwind and let myself feel the sorrow for all that was lost. When I'm at work I have to be strong for the family of employees who rely on me. On weekends I have to be strong when Steph and Stevie bring their kids over to play and share a meal. If I get misty-eyed in front of them they trade nervous glances until I force myself to stuff my emotions back down.

But for now I let myself cry, wipe my cheek with my pajama sleeve and lick the salty tears from my upper lip. The taste mingles with the smell of freshly mowed grass, and the moist smell of the earth.

The woods breathe out a coolness as the sun rises higher, and five deer prance through the trees and disappear into the shadows. Swallows dip and glide as they hunt for insects that fly up behind the mower.

As I'm finishing the last turn, a florist's van comes up the driveway and rattles to a stop. The driver emerges with a bouquet of a dozen long-stemmed red roses.

I turn off the mower and walk over to sign for the flowers. "How are you doing, Chuck?"

He holds out the roses with a knowing smile. "Looks like you have some love from above."

He's been here before, and he knows the story.

I check the card.

Love, Me

S.A.M.

Stephen Albert Milks.

"Love from above," I say.

Chuck takes my signature, salutes me with the receipt, steps in the van and drives off.

Back in the dark winter of 2006, the last time Steve was able to walk into work, he called my assistant Tonya into his office and told her to order flowers for me. "Do you remember the time the flower shop made a special arrangement for me?" he asked her. "Call them and see if they'll do another special one. I want a crutch made out of tree branches, with a nice vine to wrap up around it. Have them put flowers around the bottom."

Tonya told me later she was confused, but too upset to argue with him. "What do you want the card to say?" she asked.

There was no response. When she looked up at Steve he was staring out the window, and tears streamed down his face. "You're my crutch," he said at last, then reached for a Kleenex and blew his nose. "Fucking steroids," he muttered.

After she wrote down the order, he said "You know this flower thing has to keep going."

"What do you mean?" she asked him.

"When I'm gone. You have to keep sending them."

By then Tonya was so upset she could hardly speak. "When?"

"You'll know when," he said. "I want her to have something beautiful for holidays, birthdays, and all those "just-because" days when she might be feeling low."

The next day Tonya set up a standing order for Steve at Perkin's, my favorite florist, and I never knew a thing about it until I received the first bouquet.

Over the past four years I've received dozens of these bouquets, and they always make me feel loved. It humbles me that Steve would think about how to comfort me in the future, when he was in so much pain himself.

Sometimes the flowers make me cry, and sometimes I just stick them in a vase and try to let them be part of the background of my life, a beautiful, cheerful reminder of our history together and the love we shared.

My life goes on. I have to go on. I'm still pissed off at Steve for leaving me down here while he gets to frolic around heaven with all the good-looking angels up there. There are days when I can hardly get out of bed because I miss him so much. But who else will vacuum up dog hair from under the dining room table, if I don't get up and start cleaning? There's a new pineapple upside-down cake recipe I'm eager to try, and I still have to make sure I have enough clean platters to serve Perry and Faye when they come over for dinner tonight.

For now, though, I sit with my roses. I gather them to my heart, inhale the scent and think of the morning Steve held me in our bedroom and whispered into my hair. *When I'm gone… I'll find a way to make sure you know I love you. Because I do, Peep. I love you now, I will love you forever, and forever after that.*

The petals brush my cheek as I bow my head.

Thank you, Stephen. I love you too.

Photo Memories

Penny Milks

Penny & Steve

Photo Memories of
Their Life Together

Penny, 1974

Penny in Marching
Band Uniform

Penny at
High School Graduation, 1974

Penny's Parents, 1974

1973 Buick Riviera

Steve, 1974

Penny, 1974

Apartment complex where Steve lived in Missouri

Dorothy & Jim, 1975

Steve's Dad with Mary, Susie, Debbie & Larry in Connecticut

Stephanie & Stevie with
Candy, Sandy & Charlie, 1977

Steve relaxing with Candy on
blow-up mattress, 1976

Steve cooking at Dell Road home, 1977

Champion TransVan

Steve at Dell Road
home, 1976

Steve dressed for
work, 1976

Birthday gift from Steve

Wedding Day Breakfast
October 29, 1976

Steve & Penny cutting wedding cake

Penny's
Wedding Dress

The ring Penny made
from a quarter

1975 Buick Electra

Steve & Penny 1978

Steve's Mom at New York Townhouse

Steve & Penny, New York, 1979

Key to Steve's Heart

Bridgeman Trail House, 1980

Penny with her Mom
in the garden at Bridgeman Trail

Steve rototilling the garden

Steve in Lansing apartment with
Candy, Sandy, Charlie, Shelley, Tessy, Sugar & Jake

The All-American Dinner

Dave, 1984

Blue Pedestal Fan
1984

Steve & Penny, 1980

Steve & Penny at Dave's House, 1980

Steve
washing dishes

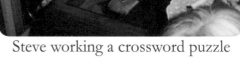

Steve working a crossword puzzle

Steve & Penny at Dave's House, 1984

Fan Prototype made of wood in 1984

Steve with Larry & Emily at RV Rally
(Larry & Emily are Fan-Tastic Vent's First Customers)

First Production Model of Fan, 1985

Steve's office at Fan-Tastic Vent, 1985

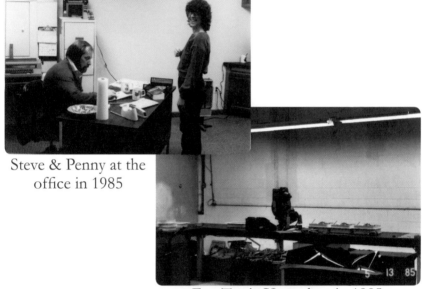

Steve & Penny at the office in 1985

Fan-Tastic Vent plant in 1985

Steve at Bus Seminar, 1987

Steve & Penny in the office
in 1986

Penny in the office, 1985

Steve's office, 1985

Jack & Buck building fans
1985

Stevie & Buck building fans
1985

Vendor Award Presentation from
RV Manufacturer, Newmar

Fleetwood
Supplier Award

Steve & Dave

1985 Stockholder's Meeting

Steve's brother, Larry

Larry's wife, Chris in 1986

Penny after hysterectomy
in 1990

Corky, Steve's baby, 1990

Father & Daughter Dance
at Stephanie's Wedding

Penny & Steve
at Stephanie's Wedding

Steve with Stephanie & Stevie in
Reno, NV at Stevie's Wedding

Fan-Tastic Vent plant in 1986
Larry's wife Chris, Buck's son Bucky & Jack's daugher Lori

Fire destroys Capac factory

No one is injured, but 47 workers are left to wonder about the future

Front Page
Newspaper Article
January 1997

The remains of the Capac plant after fire in 1997

Steve doing finish work on the
Newark Road house

Steve excavating with
the backhoe

Steve on first bulldozer,
nicknamed Baby

Waterfall pond

Steve & Penny's Newark Road Home

The view from the kitchen window

The offices after the fire

Halloween Party at
Fan-Tastic Vent

Newmar 1997 Vendor
of the Year Award

Steve at the Office
in 1989

Steve at Louisville Trade Show

Fun in Florida

Penny & Steve

Steve & Perry

Steve & his sister Susie

Penny & Faye

Perry & Faye

Penny & Steve with grandsons

Grandsons Stephen, Shea and Seth

Penny & grandson Shea

Steve & Penny with grandson Stephen

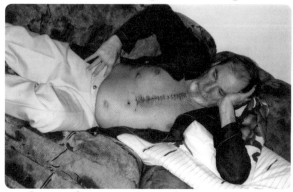

Steve after open heart bypass surgery

The Company Jet

Steve with his 1964 Plymouth

Christmas 2005

Steve & Stevie at Dave's house

Steve, Penny & Corky

Penny's Dad with "big catch" from the pond
at the Newark Road house

Penny on The Toro Mower

The weeping willow tree
in 1986

The weeping willow tree
after 10 years of growth

Steve & Penny in 1991

Steve & Penny twisting to
"Johnny Be Good"

Penny & Steve
New Year's Eve 2000

Penny & Steve
New Year's Eve 2001

Steve & Stevie in the office

Steve with rubberband moneyclip
New Year's Eve 2000

Steve & Tonya

Roses from Steve

Steve enjoying life

Steve on the Gator at the Newark Road house

Penny with her Mom & Tammie

Penny & Tammie on Gator

Penny & Tonya

Penny & Dorothy

Penny & Faye

Fan-Tastic Vent's Family of Employees

A panoramic view of Fan-Tastic Vent